Jürgen Graf

The Giant With Feet of Clay

Jürgen Graf

THE GIANT

WITH FEET OF CLAY

Raul Hilberg
and his Standard Work
on the 'Holocaust'

Theses & Dissertations Press
Capshaw 2001

HOLOCAUST Handbooks Series, Vol. 3:
Graf, Jürgen:
The Giant With Feet of Clay.
Raul Hilberg and his Standard Work on the 'Holocaust'.
Translated by Michael Humphrey
Cover: Germar Rudolf
Capshaw (Alabama): Theses & Dissertations Press, March 2001
ISBN 0-9679856-4-1
ISSN 1529-7748

Original German edition:
Graf, Jürgen:
Riese auf tönernen Füßen.
Raul Hilberg und sein Standardwerk über den 'Holocaust'.
Castle Hill Publishers, October 1999
ISBN 1-902619-02-1

Body text printed in Times New Roman, 11 pt. Throughout this book, double quotation marks ("") are used for *"quotations"* (set always in *italics*), single marks ('') for otherwise non-emphasized text of 'so-called' and 'so-to-say' character (except when used for quotations inside quotations). Quotations are introduced once with a single "-mark and ended with a "-mark (to break with the American tradition to introduce every paragraph in a quotation with a "-mark, but never closing it, which, strictly speaking, is an *"unterminated string error"*). Entire sentences or paragraphs of quoted text are rendered in 10 pt font and left indentation. Any addition to quoted text is rendered non-italic and surrounded by [brackets], so are added omission ellipses […], which could otherwise not be distinguished from ellipses in the original. Titles of books and journals are set in italics without quotation marks. References have the order: a) books: author(s)/editor(s), *title*, [volume,] [edition,] [publishing house,] town year[, pages]; b) journals: author(s), [*"title of article"*], *name of journal*, volume[(issue)] (year)[, pages] (items in brackets optional). All references to the original English version of Hilberg's book were added by the translator.

Table of Contents

"You saw, O king, and behold, a great image. This image, mighty and of exceeding brightness, stood before you, and its appearance was frightening. The head of this image was of fine. gold, its breast and arms of silver, its belly and thighs of bronze, its legs of iron, its feet partly of iron and partly of clay. As you looked, a stone was cut out by no human hand, and it smote the image on its feet of iron and clay, and broke them in pieces; then the iron, the clay, the bronze, the silver, and the gold, all together were broken in pieces, and became like the chaff of the summer threshing floors; and the wind carried them away, so that not a trace of them could be found. But the stone that struck the image became a great mountain and filled the whole earth."

– Daniel 2: 31-35 (RSV)

I. Introduction

According to the official version of history, during the Second World War the German National Socialists carried out a mass murder against the Jewish population that was unparalleled in its monstrousness and its systematic ruthlessness. Many millions of Jews, we are told, were taken from German-ruled lands and packed off to 'extermination camps' in the Polish territories and there killed, mostly in gas chambers but some in gas vans. We are also told the Germans massacred an immense number of Jews behind the eastern front. The total number of victims of gassing or shooting as well as of those who died from disease, exhaustion, hunger or other cause supposedly runs to five or six million.

This claimed unique genocide is usually labeled with the word 'Holocaust', which comes from the Greek word ὁλοκαυστός for *"entirely burned"*, and which has spread throughout and beyond the Anglo-Saxon language domain since the release of the US motion picture of the same name in 1979.

The version of the fate of the Jews during the Second World War just summarized can be found in all the dictionaries and history books of the Western world. It is taken as axiomatic in any public discussion on the 'Holocaust'. Deviation from this version is discouraged. Dissenting voices are stilled by a powerful media censorship and in many European states they are suppressed with police-state terror tactics.

In the last few decades a vast literature on the 'Holocaust' has appeared, but there is general agreement that there is one work which can be regarded as the standard work on the subject: Raul Hilberg's *The Destruction of the European Jews*.

Born in Vienna in 1926, the Jew Hilberg emigrated to the United States with his parents in 1939. In 1944 he joined the American Army. In 1948 he began to study the question of the destiny of the Jews under the National Socialist regime. In the years 1951/52 he worked in the Federal Documentation Center at Alexandria, Virginia, where his job was to evaluate captured German documents. In 1952 he was awarded a Master's degree in Political Science, and in 1955 the Doctor's degree in Law. As is the case with most other authors who have dealt with the 'Holocaust', he is not a historian by profession. However, for many years at the University of Vermont, in addition to International Relations and US Foreign Policy he has taught on the history of the Jews during the Second World War.[1]

The Destruction of the European Jews first appeared in 1961 and was reprinted unchanged in 1967 and 1979. In 1985, a *"revised and definitive"* edition with a few changes followed. Amazingly, the complete work was not published in German until 1982, and then only by a small publisher (Olle and Wolter in Berlin). It was called *Die Vernichtung der europäischen Juden*. We will use the three-volume edition published May 1997 by Fischer Taschenbuch Verlag in Frankfurt, based on the *"definitive"* English version of 1985.[2]

Hilberg's study on the 'Holocaust' claims to be the unrivalled best and most exhaustive work of its kind. This is made unmistakably clear in the introduction to the German edition of the work:

> *"If the phrase 'standard work' has any meaning at all, Hilberg's famous comprehensive history of the Holocaust must be considered as such. [...] The theme of this work is the malefactors, the plan, the method of operation and the operation itself. With the 'coolness and precision' which characterizes the great historians (Süddeutsche Zeitung) Hilberg traces the involvement and participation of the ruling elites in the government, in industry and the armed forces in the destruction of the Jews. The functional dedication of the ordinary bureaucrat, railway man, policeman and soldier to the work of annihilation will also be traced. A type of criminal steps forward (who will be named) who will never stand before a judge after 1945:*

---

1 For Hilberg's biography see the Introduction to the German edition of Hilberg's work, (*Die Vernichtung der europäischen Juden*, Fischer Taschenbuch Verlag, Frankfurt 1997), and also Barbara Kulaszka (ed.) *Did Six Million Really Die?*, Samisdat Publishers, Toronto 1992, pp. 5f. (online: http://www.ihr.org/books/kulaszka/falsenews.toc.html)

2 3 vols., Holmes and Meier, New York 1985.

the Prussian general, the national conservative ministerial official, the diplomat, the jurist, industrialists, chemists and medical doctors.

Hilberg has collected and refined the material for his book throughout his lifetime. He is known as the best-informed specialist on the sources, which for the most part came from the perpetrators. They have recorded the proof of their deadly handiwork—with characteristic thoroughness—a hundred thousand times over—with official stationery and seals.

The present comprehensive history of the Holocaust is 'source material for specialists, analysis for theoreticians and a history book without parallel for the general public.' (Sunday Times)."

That Hilberg's work is the result of an immense and devoted labor is recognized even by Revisionists, those who dispute the current version of the fate of the Jews in the Third Reich. For the Frenchman Prof. Robert Faurisson, one of the most prominent Revisionists, Hilberg stands *"high above Poliakov, Wellers, Klarsfeld and others like them."*[3] Because of Hilberg's dominant position in orthodox 'Holocaust' literature the Revisionists have had to confront his work again and again. The first such confrontation was in 1964, three years after the appearance of the first edition of *The Destruction of the European Jews.* At that time, the Frenchman Paul Rassinier, a former Resistance fighter, ex-prisoner of the NS concentration camps Buchenwald and Dora, and the founder of Revisionism, made a full attack on Hilberg. In his book *Le Drame des Juifs Européens*, Rassinier made a thorough study of Hilberg's statistics on Jewish population losses during the Second World War. He rejected the latter's conclusion that the number of Jewish victims should be set at 5.1 million; he said Hilberg could only have arrived at this number by a gross manipulation of his data. According to Rassinier, and based on Hilberg's data, the real number of Jewish NS victims was less than one million.[4]

Revisionist research has not stood still in the more than 35 years since the appearance of Rassinier's critique of Hilberg. However, there has never been a comprehensive analysis of the methods Hilberg applied nor a critical appraisal of his conclusions. The purpose of the present work is to remedy that lack.

Our investigation will concentrate on the following points:

---

3   Robert Faurisson, *"Mon expérience du révisionnisme"*, in: *Annales d'Histoire Révisionniste*, no. 8, spring 1990; quoted from Robert Faurisson, *Écrits révisionnistes (1974-1998)*, 4 volumes, privately published 1999, p. 954 (v. III). (online: http://aaargh.vho.org/fran/archFaur/1986-1990/RF9003xx1.html)

4   Paul Rassinier, *Le drame des juifs européens*, Les Sept Couleurs, Paris 1964, Reprinted by La Vieille Taupe, Paris 1984, pp. 15-32, 107-221. (online: http://aaargh.vho.org/fran/archRassi/dje/dje.html)

- What proofs does Hilberg provide that the NS regime planned the physical destruction of Jews living in its area of control?
- What proofs does Hilberg provide for the existence of extermination camps, that is, camps erected solely or partially for the murder of Jews and provided with killing gas chambers for this purpose?
- What proofs does Hilberg provide for the figure of close to 5.1 million which he claims is the number of Jewish victims of National Socialist policy?

There will be no discussion on the persecutions and deportations of Jews during the Second World War nor on the suffering of Jews in camps and ghettos, which are doubted by almost nobody: Hilberg's work rests on incontestably solid source material here. The mass shootings of Jews behind the eastern front are a different matter. It is not disputed by anyone that some shootings took place; what is in dispute by Revisionist researchers is the extent of these shootings as claimed by Hilberg and other orthodox historians. On this point too we will examine critically the numbers of victims Hilberg claims and the sources he has used.

In short, we will attempt to determine whether Hilberg's great work on the 'Holocaust' deserves the scholarly merit it lays claim to or must be found lacking.

II. General Remarks

Three points are noteworthy on a first reading of Hilberg's work:

1. Consistent Ignoring of Opposing Theses

Whoever undertook to read Hilberg's standard work without further knowledge of the problems in the study of the 'Holocaust' would never suspect that the version of events offered there is in dispute. Hilberg does not utter the least suggestion that there is a school of researchers who dispute not only the existence of a policy of extermination of the Jews in the Third Reich but also the existence of 'extermination camps' and homicidal gas chambers. Other advocates of the orthodox version of the 'Holocaust' at least mention the existence of such deviant ideas, usually only to malign them without studying them.[5] Hilberg, however, pretends he has never heard anything of the Revisionists. He pretends he has never heard of the studies of such respected and serious scholars as Arthur Butz, Wilhelm Stäglich or Robert Faurisson. Hilberg does not make mention of a single Revisionist book or a single Revisionist journal, and he does not even peripherally discuss any Revisionist objection to the annihilation thesis.

When Hilberg published the first edition of *The Destruction of the European Jews* in 1961, he could perhaps have justified ignoring viewpoints which threw doubt on the accepted version of the fate of Jews in the Third Reich; the few Revisionist works of the time were fairly modest.[6] In 1985 such a position was no longer tenable. (It is worth noting that Revisionist research has made great progress since that year while the propo-

---

5   In the introduction to the collection *Nationalsozialistische Massentötungen durch Giftgas* (Fischer Taschenbuch Verlag, Frankfurt 1986), edited by Eugen Kogon, Hermann Langbein, Adalbert Rückerl and others, the editors thunder against the *"apologists for Nazi theory and practice"* who *"deny"* the events of the past, from which in any case the reader can see that there are some who dispute the accepted version of the 'Holocaust'. Of course, neither authors nor titles are named.

6   One example is Paul Rassinier's remarkable book *Le Mensonge d'Ulysse*, which had appeared as early as 1950 (reprinted by La Vieille Taupe, Paris 1980; online: http://aaargh.vho.org/fran/ archRassi/prmu/prmu.html). However, this is a report of personal experience—necessarily colored by subjective impressions—and not a work of scholarly rigor.

nents of the extermination thesis have been marching in place and, with the sole exception of Jean-Claude Pressac, have nothing new to offer.)

Because ignoring or suppressing counter-arguments is a telltale sign of unscholarly method, considerable doubt must be cast on the credibility of Hilberg's scholarship.

2. No Photos, No Description of the Homicidal Gas Chambers and Gas Vans

Hilberg's gigantic three-volume work, running to 1,351 pages, contains exactly three photographs, namely those on the title pages of the three volumes. (*Destruction of the European Jews*, hereafter called *DEJ*, runs to 1,232 pages; there are no photographs.) In the text itself there is not one photograph, which must be considered unusual for so extensive a work. Likewise, he offers his reader no description of a gas chamber or a gas van, although this would seem to be important in view of the novelty and the monstrousness of the use of such killing machines. There is no illustration or sketch which might give inquisitive readers insight into how these gruesome instruments of murder allegedly functioned.

Hilberg's aversion to encounter the physical reality of the concentration camps and the so-called 'extermination camps' can also be seen in the fact that he has never personally undertaken an investigation at the locations of the camps. Before 1985, this man who had begun his studies on the 'Holocaust' back in 1948 had spent exactly one day in Treblinka and another half day in Auschwitz I and Auschwitz-Birkenau—*and in all three cases this was only to participate in memorial ceremonies.* He has never visited any of the other concentration camps at any time.[7] This has a very odd appearance. In contrast to Hilberg, Revisionists such as Dietlieb Felderer, Robert Faurisson, Carlo Mattogno, Germar Rudolf and the writer of these lines, and also the non-Revisionist Jean-Claude Pressac, have made thorough examinations of the buildings where the witnesses say the mass murders took place and have studied the applicable construction drawings. Such on-site research is absolutely necessary for solving this controversy.

3. Discrepancy Between the Title and the Contents of the Work

There is no doubt that the larger part of the material Hilberg presents rests on reliable sources. This applies particularly to the four hundred pages

---

7   Hilberg's statement under cross-examination by defense attorney Douglas Christie in the first Zündel trial in Toronto in 1985, cited in Barbara Kulaszka, *op. cit.* (note 1), p. 16.

in which he describes the persecution of the Jews (*Judenverfolgung*), the anti-Jewish laws and measures taken by Germany and her allies. However, the work is not entitled *The Persecution of the European Jews* (*Die Verfolgung der europäischen Juden*), but *The Destruction of the European Jews* (*Die Vernichtung der europäischen Juden*), and his title is not suitable for the work taken as a whole. Someone who has struggled through the 283 pages of the first volume has not yet encountered the subject for which Hilberg has named his work. The first 123 pages of the second volume, namely pages 287 to 410 (*DEJ*, v. 1, pages 271-390), are devoted to the "*Mobile Killing Operations*"; this concerns the mass killings behind the eastern front. No fewer than 515 pages (pp. 411 to 926; *DEJ*, v. 2, pages 391-860) deal with the deportations of Jews from areas controlled by Germany or her allies. With respect to the deportations, the facts are largely undisputed.

That which makes the 'Holocaust' so spectacular and bestial in the popular imagination, namely the industrialized slaughter in extermination camps, first shows its face on page 927; this is the beginning of the chapter on "*Killing Center Operations*" (*DEJ*, v. 3, pages 861-990). Yet the reader must persevere for another hundred pages until the subject finally comes around to the "*Killing Operations*"; in the previous five subchapters "*Origins*", "*Organization, Personnel and Maintenance*", "*Labor Utilization*", "*Medical Experiments*" and finally "*Confiscations*" in the "*Annihilation Centers*" were discussed. Remarkably, the subchapter "*Killing Operations*" is only nineteen (!!!) pages long (*DEJ*: 18); on page 1046 (*DEJ*, p. 979), the subject has already moved on to "*Liquidation of the Killing Centers and the End of the Destruction Process*".

The third volume of 290 pages is devoted entirely to "*Consequences*", "*Reflections*", "*Aftereffects*" and "*Further Developments*" before the Appendix closes the work; the latter contains Hilberg's data on Jewish population losses. (in *DEJ*, volume 3 contains the chapter on "*Killing Center Operations*") I summarize:

- 123 pages of the 1,351 page "*standard work on the Holocaust*" (*DEJ*, 120 pages of 1232 pages) deal with the killings behind the eastern front, which has received less attention both in the scholarly and in the popular literature, and which, if we are to go by Hilberg's victim counts, are also numerically less significant than the claimed mass killings in extermination camps.
- A total of 19 pages out of 1,351 (*DEJ*, 18 pages of 1232) are devoted to the central fixture of the 'Holocaust', the practical course of the claimed mass killings in gas chambers (plus there are eleven more pages on the related question of the "*Liquidation of the Killing Centers*").

- The entire first and the greater part of the second volume (in particular, the 515 pages on the deportations; in *DEJ*, most of the first volume and all the second volume containing 470 pages on deportations) have no direct bearing on the subject for which Hilberg has named his work, namely *The Destruction of the European Jews*. In the third volume, only the population statistics are applicable to our subject.

Already at this point it can be seen that the Hilberg work does not contain what the title promises. Of course, this makes the work of the critic easier in that it permits him to concentrate on a relatively small part of this large work and dispense with the rest with a few comments.

III. Remarks on the First Volume

Hilberg introduces the first chapter of his work (*"Precedents"*) with the following words:[8]

> *"The German destruction of the European Jews was a tour de force; the Jewish collapse under the German assault was a manifestation of failure. Both of these phenomena were the final product of an earlier age.*
>
> *Anti-Jewish policies and actions did not have their beginning in 1933. For many centuries, and in many countries, the Jews had been victims of destructive action."* (p. 11; *DEJ*, p. 5)

There are additional remarks on 'anti-Semitism' in European history. Hilberg regards the *"Nazi destruction process"* as the *"culmination of a cyclical trend."* In the beginning, there were attempts to convert the Jews; since they for the most part did not want to convert, expulsion was then tried, and lastly, the third, most radical method followed, the physical extermination of the Jews (pp. 14f.; *DEJ*, p. 8). Hilberg summarizes his theory by means of creative declarations:

> *"The missionaries of Christianity had said in effect: You have no right to live among us as Jews. The secular rulers who followed had proclaimed: You have no right to live among us. The German Nazis at last decreed: You have no right to live."* (p. 15; *DEJ*, p. 9)

Hilberg declares that it was no accident that enmity toward the Jews reached its most extreme pitch in Germany, since it was part of a long tradition there. In his time, Martin Luther had been a bitter opponent of the Jews, as his essay *Von den Juden und ihren Lügen* shows (On the Jews and Their Lies, published in 1543; Hilberg pp. 22ff.; *DEJ*, p. 15). From Luther Hilberg goes on to the German anti-Semites of the 19th Century and to the Jew-hating ideology of National Socialism. Next he comments on the Jewish reaction to undergoing recurring persecutions: Jews reacted to these always with *"alleviation and compliance"* (p. 34; *DEJ*, p. 27). In the Third Reich this became their doom:

---

8   To reduce the number of footnotes, whenever I cite Hilberg, the page number of the updated German version is given in parentheses. Page numbers of the English original are tagged with *DEJ*.

> *"When the Nazis took over in 1933, the old Jewish reaction pattern set in again, but this time the results were catastrophic. The German bureaucracy was not slowed by Jewish pleading; it was not stopped by Jewish indispensability. Without regard to cost, the bureaucratic machine, operating with accelerating speed and ever-widening destructive effect, proceeded to annihilate the European Jews. The Jewish community, unable to switch to resistance, increased its cooperation with the tempo of the German measures, thus hastening its own destruction.*
>
> *We see, therefore, that both perpetrators and victims drew upon their age-old experience in dealing with each other. The Germans did it with success. the Jews did it with disaster."* (p. 35; *DEJ*, p. 28)

As we see, at the beginning of his large work, Hilberg provides historical, psychological and philosophical observations on the history leading to the extermination of the Jews—*for which he has at this point provided no proof, but which he assumes to be axiomatic*. In effect, he harnesses the wagon before the horse. The proper scholarly method would have been to clarify the facts before going on to philosophize over what brought them about.

After the second chapter ("*Antecedents*") in which the anti-Jewish measures undertaken after the seizure of power of the NSDAP are described, Hilberg turns to "*The Structure of Destruction*" (pp. 56ff.; *DEJ*, pp. 51ff.). As components of the "*Destruction Process*" he includes:

- The definition of the concept 'Jew' by the National Socialists (pp. 69-84; *DEJ*, pp. 63-80) and the prohibition on the mixing of Aryans and Jews;
- The dispossession of Jews (pp. 85-163; *DEJ*, pp. 81-154);
- The concentration of Jews in designated dwelling quarters, mainly ghettos, which first affected Jews living in the area of the prewar Reich and in the Protectorates of Bohemia and Moravia and subsequently affected Jews from the Polish territories conquered in 1939.

In this chapter Hilberg relies almost exclusively on solid and accessible sources, so the facts he describes here are mostly not disputable. This part of the work constitutes a useful documentation of the step-by-step disfranchisement of the Jews under NS rule. However, there is a swindle as to names going on here that is somewhat offensive. Discrimination, dispossession and ghettoization of a minority are not components of an "*annihilation policy*". The Blacks of South Africa had no political rights under the Apartheid system and mostly lived in separated districts, yet no reasonable person would assert that they were *annihilated* by the ruling White minority. The Palestinians are tyrannized and harassed any number of ways in Israel and even more in Israeli occupied territories—they were by no means *annihilated*. Hilberg is creating a deliberate confusion of ideas.

This is not the only example of dishonesty that we encounter in the first volume. On pp. 221f. (*DEJ*, p. 212), in connection with the removal of German Jews to the East, Hilberg writes:

> *"In October 1941, mass deportations began in the Reich. They did not end until the destruction process was over. The object of these movements was not emigration but the destruction of the Jews. As yet, however, there were no killing centers in which the victims could be gassed to death, and so it was decided that, pending the construction of death camps, the Jews were to be dumped into ghettos of the incorporated territories and the occupied Soviet areas further east. The target in the incorporated territories was the ghetto of Łódź."*

Hilberg still owes his readers a proof for this assertion. While the entire process of the removal of German Jews to the East can be documented up one side and down the other—and Hilberg mostly relies on German original documents in his numerous footnotes—he does not cite any document as source for the above assertion, nor even any witness testimony.

The passage just cited is one of the first clear examples of a dishonest tactic that Hilberg employs frequently in the second volume: He embeds undocumented assertions (or assertions supported only by questionable witness testimony) on *annihilation of Jews* among properly documented statements on *persecution of Jews* or *deportation of Jews* and may have hoped that the reader will not catch him. In the case above the illogic of his assertion can be grasped with both hands, especially when regarded in context. On pages 215-225 (*DEJ*, 205-214), Hilberg describes the logistical and organizational difficulties caused by the improvised mass removals of German Jews to the West Polish territories incorporated into the Reich in 1939 and to the *Generalgouvernement* and how furiously the local NS authorities opposed these removals. For example, Werner Ventzki, Chief Mayor of the city of Łódź, renamed Litzmannstadt, protested vehemently against the plan Reichsführer SS Heinrich Himmler was considering in September 1941 to deport 20,000 Jews and 5,000 gypsies to the Łódź ghetto, from which they were to be shipped further East the following year. Ventzki insisted that the arrival of 25,000 more persons in the ghetto, which was already full to overflowing, would raise the density of occupation to seven persons per room, that the new arrivals would have to be lodged in factories, which would disrupt production, that people would starve and that it would be impossible to prevent epidemics (pp. 222f.; *DEJ*, pp. 212f.). Nevertheless, the removal went forward.

If the purpose of the deportations was "*not emigration but the destruction of the Jews*", as Hilberg asserts, the National Socialist policy of removal of the Jews to the East before the completion of the 'death camps' becomes senseless. According to Hilberg's book, the two first 'death camps', Chełmno and Bełżec, became operational in December 1941 and in March 1942, respectively (p. 956; *DEJ*, p. 893). In that case, I ask: why would the Germans send massive numbers of Jews into the ghettos starting in October 1941 to wait for the 'death camps' to become operational, instead of holding off on the deportations for three or four months to save themselves the organizational headaches and the chaos in the ghettos? Hilberg does not bother to discuss obvious questions of this sort.

Nevertheless, the first volume of *The Destruction of the European Jews* represents a well-researched documentation on the destiny of the Jews in the Third Reich from 1933 to 1941. People may disagree as to the interpretation of the facts—but we are interested only in the facts themselves, and, unlike Hilberg, we refrain from random philosophizing. It is an abuse for Hilberg to classify the measures taken by the NS regime during this period as "*annihilation policy*"—they clearly do not fall under that heading.

IV. The Lack of Documents on Annihilation Policy and its Consequences for the Orthodox Historians

1. *"No Documents Have Survived"*

That no one has ever found a written order for the physical extermination of the Jews originating with Adolf Hitler or any other leading NS politician is agreed upon by historians of all orientations. Léon Poliakov, one of the most prominent proponents of the orthodox picture of the 'Holocaust', stated unequivocally:[9]

> *"The archives of the Third Reich and the depositions and accounts of its leaders make possible a reconstruction, down to the last detail, of the origin and development of the plans for aggression, the military campaigns, and the whole array of procedures by which the Nazis intended to reshape the world to their liking. Only the campaign to exterminate the Jews, as regards its conception as well as many other essential aspects, remains shrouded in darkness. Inferences, psychological considerations, and third- or fourth-hand reports enable us to reconstruct its development with considerable accuracy. Certain details, however, must remain forever unknown. The three or four people chiefly involved in the actual drawing up of the plan for total extermination are dead and no documents have survived, perhaps none ever existed."*

Nothing needs to be changed in this statement. At a congress of historians held in Stuttgart in 1984 covering *"The Murder of the Jews in the Second World War"*, the participants reached agreement on only one point, namely that a written order for the annihilation had never been found.[10]

This circumstance has caused historical researchers headaches for a long time. A gigantic operation such as the deportation of several millions of Jews into 'extermination camps' and their murder there necessarily presupposes an organization which must have involved the participation of thousands upon thousands of persons, and such a thing does not happen

---

9   Léon Poliakov, *Harvest of Hate*, Holocaust Library, New York 1979, p. 108.
10   Eberhard Jäckel and Jürgen Rohwer (eds.), *Der Mord an den Juden im Zweiten Weltkrieg*, Deutsche Verlagsanstalt, Stuttgart 1985, p. 186.

without written orders—especially not in such a bureaucratically organized state as the Third Reich was. The National Socialists mostly did not destroy their documents as the war came to an end; rather, these fell in huge amounts into the hands of the victors. In his well-known book *Rise and Fall of the Third Reich*,[11] William L. Shirer describes how this resulted in:

> "[…] the capture of most of the confidential archives of the German government and all its branches, including those of the Foreign Office, the Army, the Navy, the National Socialist Party and Heinrich Himmler's secret police. Never before, I believe, has such a vast treasure fallen into the hands of contemporary historians. […] The swift collapse of the Third Reich in spring of 1945 resulted in the surrender not only of a vast bulk of its secret papers but of other priceless material such as private diaries, highly secret speeches, conference reports and correspondence, and even transcripts of telephone conversations of the NS leaders tapped by a special office set up by Hermann Göring in the Air Ministry. […] 485 tons of records of the German Foreign Office, captured by the U.S. First Army in various castles and mines in the Harz Mountains just as they were about to be burned on orders from Berlin […] Hundreds of thousands of captured documents were hurriedly assembled at Nuremberg as evidence in the trial of the major war criminals."

In view of this mountain of NS documents, the lack of any documentary proof for a policy of annihilation of the Jews is painfully embarrassing for the proponents of the official picture of the 'Holocaust'. The argument that at least in the 'extermination camps' the incriminating papers were destroyed in time is useless, especially since 1991: In that year the Soviets made available to Western researchers the documents of the Central Construction Office in Auschwitz captured by the Red Army in 1945. The Central Construction Office was an organization that was responsible for the construction of the crematories—the crematories which supposedly contained the gas chambers for the mass killing of Jews. There are no less than 88,000 pages of documents.[12] They do not contain any evidence for the construction of homicidal gas chambers. If there had been, the Communists would have announced it to the world triumphantly in 1945.

The complete lack of documentary evidence for a policy of annihilation of the Jews as well as for the construction of gas chambers for killing purposes has led to a split in the ranks of the orthodox historians, meaning those who uphold the theory of the deliberate and systematic annihilation of

---

11 William L. Shirer, *Rise and Fall of the Third Reich*, Simon and Schuster, New York, 1960, pp. ix, x.
12 During two extended visits to Moscow in 1995 together with Italian historian Carlo Mattogno we examined 88,000 pages and made copies of 4,000 of them.

the Jews, between Intentionalists and Functionalists. In what follows we will compare the two orientations.

2. Intentionalists and Functionalists

At a colloquium on *"Nazi Germany and the Genocide of the Jews"* held at the Sorbonne in Paris in 1982, US historian Christopher Browning summarized the difference of opinion between Intentionalists and Functionalists with respect to the genesis of the policy of annihilation of the Jews as follows:[13]

> *"In recent years the interpretations of National Socialism have polarized more and more into two groups that Tim Mason has aptly called 'Intentionalists' and 'Functionalists'. The former explain the development of Nazi Germany as a result of Hitler's intentions, which came out of a coherent and logical ideology and were realized due to an all-powerful totalitarian dictatorship. The 'Functionalists' point out the anarchistic character of the Nazi state, its internal rivalries and the chaotic process of decision-making, which constantly led to improvisation and radicalization […] These two modes of exposition of history are useful for the analysis of the strongly divergent meanings that people attribute to the Jewish policy of the Nazis in general and to the Final Solution in particular. On the one hand, Lucy Dawidowicz, a radical Intentionalist, upholds the viewpoint that already in 1919 Hitler had decided to exterminate European Jews. And not only that: He knew at what point in time his murderous plan would be realized. The Second World War was at the same time the means and opportunity to put his 'war against the Jews' into effect. While he waited for the anticipated moment for the realization of his 'great plan', naturally he tolerated a senseless and meaningless pluralism in the Jewish policies of the subordinate ranks of state and party.*
>
> *Against the radical Intentionalism of Lucy Dawidowicz, which emphasizes the intentions and 'great plan' of Hitler, the Ultrafunctionalism of Martin Broszat constitutes a diametrically opposed view of the role of the Führer, especially with respect to the decision on the Final Solution. It is Broszat's position that Hitler never took a definitive decision nor issued a general order for the Final Solution. The annihilation program developed in stages in conjunction with a series of isolated massacres at the end of 1941 and in 1942. These locally limited mass murders were improvised answers to an impossible situation that had developed as a result of two factors: First the ideological and political pressure for the creation of a 'Jew-free' Europe that stemmed from Hitler and then the military reverses on the east-*

---

13 Christopher Browning, *"La décision concernant la solution finale"*, in: *Colloque de l'Ecole des Hautes Etudes en sciences sociales, L'Allemagne nazie et le génocide juif*, Gallimard-Le Seuil, Paris 1985, pp. 191f.

ern front that led to stoppages in railway traffic and caused the buffer zones into which the Jews were to be removed to disappear. Once the annihilation program was in progress, it gradually institutionalized itself until it was noticed that it offered the simplest solution logistically and became a program universally applied and single-mindedly pursued. From this standpoint, Hitler was a catalyst but not a decision-maker.

For Lucy Dawidowicz the Final Solution was thought out twenty years before it was put into practice; For Martin Broszat the idea developed from practice—sporadic murders of groups of Jews led to the idea to kill all Jews systematically."

The constructions described by Browning of Lucy Dawidowicz and Martin Broszat as extreme representatives of the Intentionalists and the Functionalists are both equally untenable.

First as to the theory propounded by Lucy Dawidowicz that the extermination of the Jews was the *"great plan"* of Hitler long before his accession to power. If this were so, Hitler would never have pursued for years on end a single-minded demand for Jewish emigration. It is undisputed that NS policy during the six years of peace that the Third Reich enjoyed was directed at motivating as many Jews as possible to emigrate. To achieve this aim, as is well known, the National Socialists worked closely with Zionist forces, who were interested in the settlement of as many Jews as possible in Palestine.[14] However, the number of Jews who were willing to risk an uncertain future in the Orient was limited.

Raul Hilberg has described in detail how intensively the National Socialists pushed Jewish emigration. He relates how the National Socialists exerted themselves to persuade ten thousand Polish Jews who still lived in Germany in 1938 (!) to return to Poland and how the latter refused to take back its Jewish fellow citizens (p. 413; *DEJ*, p. 394). One should take note that after five years of Hitler's rule ten thousand Polish Jews preferred conditions in the anti-Semitic Third Reich to those of their native Poland!

At the time of Hitler's accession to power 520,000 Jews lived in Germany. Due to emigration and an excess of deaths over births, by 1938 their number had dwindled to 350,000, but the *Anschluss* with Austria brought an additional 190,000 Austrian Jews (p. 412; *DEJ*, p. 394). In response, on 26th August 1938 Reichskommissar Bürckel—he had administrative responsibility for the reunion of Austria and the Reich—set up a *"Central Office for Jewish Emigration"*. Bürckel's method was soon followed throughout the Reich. On 24th January 1939 Göring ordered the founding

---

14 On National Socialist-Zionist cooperation see, for example, Edwin Black, *The Transfer Agreement*, New York-London 1994; Francis Nicosia, *Hitler und der Zionismus*, Druffel Verlag, Leoni 1989.

of a Reich Central Office for Jewish Emigration and put Reinhard Heydrich in charge (pp. 414f.; *DEJ*, p. 396).

The beginning of war did not alter the fundamental direction of National Socialist Jewish policy. Naturally, the difficulties were magnified by the fact that the number of Jews had grown by the addition of a massive number of foreign, mainly Polish, Jews. The German area of influence in Europe could now no longer be made 'Jew-free' (*judenrein*)—this is the National Socialist term—by individual emigration. Therefore the NS leaders turned their attention to the Madagascar Plan. On this subject Raul Hilberg comments:

> "*The Madagascar Project was designed to take care of millions of Jews. The authors of the plan wanted to empty the Reich-Protektorate area and all of occupied Poland of their Jewish population.* [...]
>
> *But the Madagascar Plan did not materialize. It hinged on the conclusion of a peace treaty with France, and such a treaty depended on an end of hostilities with England.* [...]
>
> *Even as it faded, the project was to be mentioned one more time, during early February 1941, in Hitler's headquarters. On that occasion, the party's labor chief, Ley, brought up the Jewish question and Hitler, answering at length, pointed out that the war was going to accelerate the solution of this problem but that he was also encountering additional difficulties. Originally he had been in a position to address himself at most to the Jews of Germany, but now the goal had to be the elimination of Jewish influence in the entire Axis power sphere* [...] *He was going to approach the French about Madagascar. When Bormann asked how the Jews could be transported there in the middle of the war, Hitler replied that one would have to consider that. He would be willing to make available the entire German fleet for this purpose, but he did not wish to expose his crews to the torpedoes of enemy submarines.*" (pp. 416f.; *DEJ*, pp. 397f.)

Had Hitler, as Lucy Dawidowicz and other Intentionalists claim, planned for the extermination of the Jews and even foreseen that this goal could be achieved in the framework of a world war, he would never have made any efforts to encourage Jewish emigration and would have blocked any such efforts especially after the war had begun. There would never have been anything like a Madagascar Plan sponsored by the NS leadership. Emigrated Jews are not subject to extermination.

The opposing theory, that of the radical Functionalists around Broszat, stands in irreconcilable contradiction with the claims of the adherents of the theory of Jewish annihilation and also with other claims of the Functionalists themselves.

As Browning summarized in his presentation at the 1982 Paris Colloquium, Broszat believes that local massacres of Jews led to the plan to kill all Jews; thus the idea developed from the practical situation itself. The military reverses on the eastern front had caused the buffer zones to disappear in which it was intended to remove the Jews. This contradicts the view held by the orthodox historians that the mass murders behind the eastern front began in earnest immediately after the German invasion of the Soviet Union. The largest of the claimed mass shootings, that of Babi Yar near Kiev, supposedly happened on 29th September 1941, at a time when the Wehrmacht had suffered no significant reverses. All Jews in Kiev the Germans could get their hands on, in total more than 33,000, were supposedly shot in Babi Yar. In the following months tens of thousands more Jewish victims allegedly followed them.[15]

One cannot exclude that there were shootings of Jews shortly after the beginning of the German-Soviet War, and we will discuss this question in the next chapter. For the most part they were reprisals for attacks of partisans against German troops. (The *"Commissar Order"* for the shooting of Jewish-Bolshevist commissars is not pertinent here, because it deals with the killing of individual persons identified by function and not the indiscriminate slaughter of civilians because of their 'race'.) A monstrous bloodbath like that claimed for Babi Yar could never have happened without the permission of the highest authority. No local commander would have dared to undertake a measure fraught with such heavy consequences without assurance of support from higher authority. Thus, the alleged murder of *all* Jews remaining in Kiev after the Germans entered would only be conceivable as a component of a planned extermination policy. Also, if the Babi Yar story is true, such a policy must have already existed by the end of September 1941.

Let us pursue this argument further. Chełmno (Kulmhof in German) is supposed to have been opened as the first 'extermination camp' in December 1941 (Hilberg, p. 956; *DEJ*, p. 893). If Hilberg is right, the order to build it must have been issued some time before, because a camp does not spring up overnight. Now it is not possible that some random local German authorities decided on their own account to build an extermination camp. But here also, the existence of an order from higher authority is an absolute precondition.

This implies the bankruptcy of Broszat's Functionalist theory, in which the Holocaust comes about as the result of the first German reverses

---

15 For the official description of Babi Yar see E.R. Wien, *Die Shoa von Babi Jar*, Hartung-Gorre, Constance 1991. Hilberg mentions the supposed massacre on p. 311 (*DEJ*, p. 297) and other places.

on the eastern front, and we come back to the intentionalist question: When did the order to exterminate the Jews go out?

In his presentation at the Paris Colloquium, Christopher Browning added the following to his description of the theories of Lucy Dawidowicz and Martin Broszat:[16]

> *"Between these two extreme poles there are a number of positions occupying interpretive middle ground. Eberhard Jäckel believes the idea for the killing of the Jews came to Hitler some time around 1924. Karl Dietrich Bracher emphasizes Hitler's threatening declarations at the end of the '30's and believes his intentions were already settled. Andreas Hillgruber and Klaus Hildebrand maintain that ideological factors were controlling, but do not propose any firm date. Others, and not Functionalists only, believe the decisive point was in 1941; Léon Poliakov thinks that the beginning of 1941 is the most probable point, while Robert Kempner and Helmut Krausnick hold the opinion that Hitler made the decision in the spring, while preparations for the invasion of Russia were under way. […] Uwe Dietrich Adam inclines to the idea that the decision was taken in the fall, at a time when the military offensive had stalled and the 'territorial solution' through mass expulsion to Russia became impossible. Finally, Sebastian Haffner, who is certainly no Functionalist, defends the date of the beginning of December, when the first foreboding of a military defeat drove Hitler to strive for an irrevocable victory over the Jews."*

These observations expose with harsh clarity the chronological travesties by the orthodox 'Holocaust' historians, which reduce them to idle, conspiratorial speculations in cuckoo land. *All* the proposed dates lack any serious foundation, in that there is not one with any documentary support. Instead of indulging in useless speculation as to a point in time when the annihilation of the Jews was decided upon, these academics would have done better to study the question first, whether such a thing ever existed. This cardinal question was prudently avoided at the Paris historians' congress as well as at the Stuttgart historians' congress held two years later. At the latter as well, the question of the date when the fateful decision was made was tortured to death. The congress participants came no nearer an answer then than two years before in Paris.

It is notable that none of the researchers named by Browning held to the old fairy tale that the decision for the annihilation of the Jews was taken at the Wannsee Conference in Berlin on 20th January 1942. In 1992 the Israeli 'Holocaust' expert Yehuda Bauer derided this tough old myth as a *"silly story."*[17]

---

16 Christopher Browning, *op. cit.* (note 13) p. 192.
17 *Canadian Jewish News*, 30th January 1992.

3. Raul Hilberg's Errors and Confusions

a. Was There the Ominous Hitler Order or Not?

On the cardinal question, whether Hitler ever gave an express order for the physical extinction of the Jews present in his area of control, Hilberg gives different answers in the first and in the revised edition of his work. In the first edition published in 1961 he asserted that there had been two successive Hitler orders to this effect, the first regarding the killing of Russian Jews and the second regarding the annihilation of all other Jews living under German rule. He gave no documentary proof for these orders. We quote the relevant passage:[18]

> "How was the killing phase brought about? Basically, we are dealing with two of Hitler's decisions. One order was given in the spring of 1941, during the planning of the invasion of the USSR; it provided that small units of the SS and Police be dispatched to Soviet territory, where they were to move from town to town to kill all Jewish inhabitants on the spot. This method may be called the 'mobile killing operations'. Shortly after the mobile operations had begun in the occupied Soviet territories, Hitler handed down his second order. That decision doomed the rest of European Jewry."

In the second and "*definitive*" edition which appeared in 1985, on which the German translation we use was based, both of these phantom orders disappear without a trace. Christopher Browning, to his credit, remarked on this in an article written in 1986:[19]

> "In the new edition, all references in the text to a Hitler decision or Hitler order for the 'Final Solution' [which Browning understands to mean physical extermination] have been systematically excised."

This is a devastating blow to Hilberg's credibility! Of course, Hilberg still assumes that Hitler had initiated the annihilation of the Jews. In 1985, he wrote:

> "For years, the administrative machine had taken its initiatives and engaged in its forays one step at a time. In the course of that evolution, a direction had been charted and a pattern had been established. By the middle of 1941, the dividing line had been reached, and beyond it lay a field of unprecedented actions unhindered by the limits of the past. More and more of the participants were on the verge of realizing the nature of what could happen now. Salient in this crystallization was the role of Adolf Hitler him-

---

18 Raul Hilberg, *The Destruction of the European Jews*, Quadrangle Books, Chicago 1967, p. 177. This is an unchanged reprint of the first edition published in 1961. We thank Robert Faurisson for pointing out the mention of the supposed Hitler order as well as sending the pages involved.

19 Christopher Browning, "*The Revised Hilberg*", in: *Simon Wiesenthal Center Annual*, 1986, p. 294.

self, his stance before the world and, more specifically, his wishes or expectations voiced in an inner circle." (p. 420; *DEJ*, pp. 401f.)

Behind these turgid passages hides the presupposition that Hitler personally commanded the annihilation of the Jews. One could therefore describe Hilberg as a 'moderate Intentionalist'. The informant upon whom he relies is Adolf Eichmann. The latter wrote in his memoirs that at the turn of the year 1941/1942 Reinhard Heydrich, chief of the RSHA, told him that the Führer had decreed the physical destruction of the Jews.[20] Hilberg says this in footnote 30 on pp. 420f. (*DEJ*, p. 402), and continues:

> *"During his interrogation by Israeli police in Jerusalem, he* [Eichmann] *suggested more plausibly that Hitler's order had come two or three months after the June 22 German assault on the USSR. [...] Chronology and circumstances point to a Hitler decision before the summer ended."*

That such a crucial statement could be relegated to a footnote gives some inkling of Hilberg's helpless perplexity! Hilberg now relies on a suggestion(!) from Eichmann, who himself relied on alleged hearsay evidence!

At the Stuttgart Congress in 1984 Hilberg again opined that Hitler had given the decision for the extermination of the Jews—naturally, only verbally!—in summer 1941.[21] The date given by Hilberg is after February 1941, when the Madagascar Plan was seriously considered for the last time, but before the claimed massacre of Babi Yar and the alleged beginning of operations of the 'extermination camp' Chełmno. By so doing, Hilberg avoided the radical impossibilities on which the theories of Lucy Dawidowicz and Martin Broszat were so weakly founded.

Just as little as Dawidowicz, Broszat and all other Intentionalist and Functionalist 'Holocaust' historians, Hilberg cannot produce even a single document to support his hypothesis. Moreover, he contradicts himself in that he repeatedly conjures up an *"annihilation policy"*, an *"annihilation process"* and *"annihilation machinery"* before the beginning of the German-Soviet war. In connection with the last deliberations by Hitler on the Madagascar Plan that happened in February 1941, he writes:

> *"While Hitler was thinking, the machinery of destruction was permeated with a feeling of uncertainty. In the Generalgouvernement, where ghettoization was viewed as a transitional measure, the unsightly Jewish quarters with their impoverished crowds were trying the patience of local German officials. These irritations and frustrations were expressed in monthly reports by the late summer of 1940. In the Lublin District the Kreishauptmann of Kranystaw, surfeited with his administrative tasks,* [in Sep-

---

20 Adolf Eichmann, *Ich, Adolf Eichmann*, Druffel Verlag, Leoni 1980, p. 479.
21 E. Jäckel, J. Rohwer (eds.), *op. cit.* (note 10), p. 126.

tember 1940] *insisted that Jews who had Polonized their names spell them in German—in Madagascar, he said, they could have Madagascarian names.[20]"* (p. 417; *DEJ*, p. 399)

If a) Hitler decided on the annihilation of the Jews in August or September 1941 and b) local German officials were predicting for the Jews a future in Madagascar in September 1940, it makes no sense to talk about a *"machinery of destruction"* existing in September 1940.

Elementary, my dear Watson!

b. *"No Special Agency... No Special Budget"*

An annihilation policy necessarily presupposes a mechanism for its execution, and this mechanism must needs be held in the hands of a central authority invested with the requisite powers. But no, Hilberg says there was no such thing; already in the first volume he has written:

> *"In the final analysis, the destruction of the Jews was not so much a product of laws and commands as it was a matter of spirit, of shared comprehension, of consonance and synchronization.*
>
> *Who shared in this undertaking? What kind of machinery was used for these tasks? The machine of destruction was an aggregate—no one agency was charged with the whole operation. […]*
>
> *No special agency was created and no special budget was devised to destroy the Jews of Europe. Each organization was to play a specific role in the process, and each was to find the means to carry out its task."* (pp. 58, 66; *DEJ*, pp. 55, 62)

Picture that: a project for a mammoth undertaking—complicated by the conditions of war—including the construction of 'extermination camps' and the deportation of millions of persons from every which country into the camps—and this all should be done without a responsible central authority, a special office or a special budget!

Raul Hilberg took part in the Paris Historian's Congress in 1982; the subject of his presentation was *"The Bureaucracy of the Final Solution"*. Hilberg revealed what would have been necessary to carry out the annihilation of the Jews, namely, 1) railroads, 2) police, and especially 3) dedicated bureaucrats.[22]

How sophisticated! When a state has decided to deport millions of persons from any country by train to death factories and then to kill them there, it would in fact need railroads to carry the trains, it would certainly need policemen to guard the condemned, and its bureaucrats should not be

---

22　Hilberg's paper is included in *L'Allemagne nazie et le génocide juif, op. cit.* (note 13), pp. 219ff.

too tender-hearted. One does not have to be a professor at the University of Vermont to understand this nor to have written the standard work on the 'Holocaust'. The banalities hawked by Hilberg do not in any way replace the missing proof of an extermination policy.

c. The Myth of the Code Language

Lacking documentary proof for a German policy of annihilation of the Jews, Hilberg resorts to a dodge, one that has enjoyed great popularity among orthodox 'Holocaust' scholars for a long time and whose origin can be traced back to the Nuremberg Trials. The Italian researcher Carlo Mattogno characterizes it as follows:[23]

> *"The Nuremberg inquisitors invented [...] this roundabout method of speaking, which consisted in reading into any particular document that which one wanted it to say. This method is the basis for the—arbitrary and unfounded—assumption that the high NS authorities used a form of code language even in their most secret documents, which the Nuremberg inquisitors naturally claimed they had the key to. This was the reason for the systematic twisting of the meaning of otherwise quite innocent documents for the purpose of supporting the extermination theory."*

Here is an example. Along with the Wannsee Conference, at which Hitler's decision to annihilate the Jews was to be disclosed to an at first small circle of NS bureaucrats—this is Hilberg's version of the purpose of this conference—supposedly,

> *"Gradually the news of the 'Final Solution' seeped through the ranks of the bureaucracy. The knowledge did not come to all officials at once. How much a man knew depended on his proximity to the destructive operations and on his insight into the nature of the destruction process. Seldom, however, was comprehension recorded on paper. When the bureaucrats had to deal with deportation matters, they kept referring to a 'Jewish migration'. In official correspondence the Jews were still 'wandering'. They were 'evacuated' (evakuiert) and 'resettled' (umgesiedelt, ausgesiedelt). They 'wandered off' (wanderten ab) and 'disappeared' (verschwanden). These terms were not the product of naïveté, but convenient tools of psychological repression."* (p. 425; *DEJ*, p. 406)

That expressions such as "*resettle*" (*aussiedeln*), "*evacuate*" (*evakuieren*) and so forth can only be code language for 'kill' is, of course, nothing but an allegation. Moreover, even Hilberg had to admit that even after the supposed Hitler decision to exterminate the Jews, many Jews were removed to the occupied territories in the East, which one may certainly describe as

---

23 Carlo Mattogno, *La soluzione finale. Problemi e polemiche*, Edizioni di Ar, Padua 1991, pp. 64f.

'resettlement' (*Aussiedlung*). For example, he relates the deportation of German Jews to Riga and Minsk (p. 369; *DEJ*, p. 352). Germany's worsening circumstances in the war made the continuance of this policy impossible. If the authorities had wanted to kill these German Jews, there could have been no good reason to haul them off to Latvia and White Russia in the always urgently needed trains instead of killing them in Germany itself or sending them to one of the 'extermination camps' even then (November 1941) supposedly being built in Poland.

It hardly needs to be mentioned that for Hilberg the term "*final solution*" (*Endlösung*) stands as a synonym for 'extermination' (*Ausrottung*). For example, this is the sense in which he interprets Göring's well-known letter to Heydrich on 31st July 1942, frequently quoted in the literature on the subject, in which the former orders the latter to submit, "*in the near future an overall plan of the organizational, functional and material measures to be taken in preparing for the implementation of the aspired final solution of the Jewish question*".[24] Hilberg adds, Heydrich now held "*the reins of the destruction process in his hands*" (p. 420; *DEJ*, p. 401). Göring's expression, that Heydrich should "*undertake, by emigration or evacuation, a solution of the Jewish question as advantageous as possible under the conditions at the time*", Hilberg interprets the same way as his predecessors from Poliakov to Reitlinger as code language for physical annihilation. No serious historian who wrote on an era other than the Third Reich and the Second World War would be permitted to distort the statements of his original sources so capriciously.

That the National Socialists took "*final solution of the Jewish question*" (*Endlösung der Judenfrage*) to mean the expulsion (*Ausweisung*) or removal (*Abschiebung*) of all Jews from Europe, can be shown by a number of documents. For example, Franz Rademacher, official in charge of Jewish affairs in the Germany Section of the Foreign Office on 10th February 1942, and thus at a time when according to Hilberg the mass murder was allegedly in full swing, and Bełżec, following Chełmno, was close to opening as the second extermination camp, wrote a letter to a Herr Bielfeld of the Foreign Ministry in which he stated that the Führer had decided that "*the Jews should be removed not to Madagascar, but to the East*", and added, "*Madagascar will no longer be needed for the final solution*".[25] Not even the Giant Raul Hilberg has dared to claim that the Germans planned to gas the Jews in

---

24 PS-710.
25 NG-5770.

the jungles of Madagascar. And why does Hilberg omit such major pieces of documentary evidence?

d. Hitler Quotation as 'Proof' for the Mass Murder

As do other proponents of the orthodox picture of the 'Holocaust', Hilberg interprets statements by Adolf Hitler in which he threatens the Jews with *"annihilation"* (*Vernichtung*) or *"extermination"* (*Ausrottung*) as proof that such a thing really happened. He quotes (on p. 425; *DEJ*, p. 407) a Hitler speech of 30th September 1942 in which the Reichschancellor stated as follows:[26]

> *"In my Reichstag speech of September 1, 1939, I have spoken of two things: first, that now that the war has been forced upon us, no array of weapons and no passage of time will bring us to defeat, and second, that if Jewry should plot another world war to exterminate [zur Ausrottung] the Aryan peoples of Europe, it would not be the Aryan peoples which would be exterminated, [ausgerottet] but Jewry. [...] At one time, the Jews of Germany laughed about my prophecies. I do not know whether they are still laughing or whether they have already lost all desire to laugh. But right now I can only repeat: they will stop laughing everywhere, and I shall be right also in that prophecy."*

It needs to be noted that a warlike way of speaking was characteristic of the National Socialists, who before coming to power had to prevail against their adversaries on the extreme left in countless clashes in meeting rooms and streets. It should also be remembered that wild threats against an enemy in wartime are common. But the important point is a semantic one. In present usage, *ausrotten* means only 'to physically liquidate', but formerly the word—whose etymology is 'uproot'—had a broader meaning. Thus in *Mein Kampf* Adolf Hitler wrote the following on conditions in the Danube Monarchy before the First World War:[27]

> *"Immense were the burdens which the German people were expected to bear, inconceivable their sacrifices in taxes and blood, and yet anyone who was not totally blind was bound to recognize that all this would be in vain. What pained us most was the fact that this entire system was morally whitewashed by the alliance with Germany, with the result that the slow extermination [Ausrottung] of Germandom in the old monarchy was in a certain sense sanctioned by Germany itself."*

Now Hitler certainly did not mean to say that old Kaiser Franz Josef planned to gas or shoot all the German Austrians, but rather that they ran the

---

26 *Völkischer Beobachter*, 30th September 1942.
27 Adolf Hitler, *Mein Kampf*, Franz Eher Verlag, Munich 1933, pp. 13f.

danger of losing their power to the Slavs. *Ausrotten* clearly possessed the meaning 'deprive of power, rob of influence.'

The reader should also remember that on 1st September 1939 Hitler criticized the Jews for wanting to let loose a world war for the *"elimination of the Aryan peoples"* (*Ausrottung der arischen Völker*). It cannot be seriously contended that he meant to say the Jews intended the eradication of the entire population of Europe root and branch. Here again *"Ausrottung"* means 'subjection' or 'deprivation of power'. This meaning applies to all such endlessly distorted Hitler quotations in the 'Holocaust' literature.

e. Two Insoluble Problems

As do all other radical or moderate Intentionalists, Hilberg faces two insuperable problems which he simply ignores:

1. If the National Socialists had decided at any time on the physical liquidation of Jews present in their area of control, from that time forward there would be no documents which spoke of deployment of Jewish labor. However, such documents exist in large numbers. We will quote from a few of them later in discussing the deportations.[28] The following problem is even more insoluble for the Intentionalists:

2. If there had been a systematic policy of annihilation of the Jews there would have been effectively no Jews left in the territories in the control of the Third Reich. Every Jew the Germans could have gotten their hands on would have been killed and the few survivors would have had to ascribe their survival to 'chance' or 'miracle'. In reality, the majority of the Jewish population in the countries occupied by the Third Reich avoided any deportation. It is well-known that from France only slightly more than 20% of the Jews were deported, most of whom were foreigners and lacked proper identification. Jews with French passports were mostly left alone. The same applies to those with Belgian passports. Under any extermination policy there would have been effectively none who returned and we would not have on hand the uncounted 'testimonies of Holocaust survivors' that now fill whole libraries.[29]

---

28 Cf. chapter VI.2.

29 According to Israeli sources, there were some 1,000,000 'Holocaust survivors' still alive in 1998, which equals some 4-5 million 'survivors' in 1945! Cf. Germar Rudolf, *"Holocaust Victims: A Statistical Analysis. W. Benz and W. N. Sanning—a Comparison"*; in: E. Gauss (ed.), *Dissecting the Holocaust*, Theses & Dissertations Press, Capshaw, AL, 2000, p. 211ff. (online: http://codoh.com/found/fndstats.html)

f. *"An Incredible Meeting of Minds"*

In February 1983 Raul Hilberg had the effrontery to write:[30]

> *"[…] what began in 1941 was a process of destruction not planned in advance, not organized centrally by any agency. There was no blueprint and there was no budget for destructive measures. They were taken step by step, one step at a time. Thus came not so much a plan being carried out, but an incredible meeting of minds, a consensus-mind reading by a far-flung bureaucracy."*

Robert Faurisson pointed out these pearls of Hilbergian interpretive art and sarcastically commented that in his own experience the last thing one could ever expect from a bureaucracy was a meeting of minds and telepathy.[31]

Difficilis est satiram non *scribere*—it is difficult *not* to write satire. It would be difficult to find any clearer display anywhere than these few sentences of the total bankruptcy of the orthodox historiography of the 'Holocaust', together with their figurehead, the Giant with feet of clay.

---

30 *Newsday*, Long Island/New York, 23rd February 1983, p. II/3.
31 Robert Faurisson, *Écrits révisionnistes, op. cit.* (note 3), p. 959.

V. The Massacres Behind the Eastern Front

1. The Initial Situation

On 22nd June 1941, the Wehrmacht marched into the USSR. The official version of history has it that this was an unprovoked attack. On the other hand, Revisionists such as the Russian historian Suvorov and the German historian Hoffmann maintain that by doing so, Hitler was able to forestall an impending Soviet attack.[32]

In the territories taken by the Germans, Soviet partisans stirred up a bloody underground war which took the lives of many German soldiers. The Soviets boasted that their partisans had killed 500,000 members of the German army.[33] The Germans reacted to these actions—which violated international law—the way other occupying powers before and since have done, with severe reprisal measures even against the civilian population.[34] Many civilians were shot as hostages, whole villages were burned to the ground.

---

32 Victor Suvorov, *Icebreaker: Who Started the Second World War?*, Hamish Hamilton, London 1990; V. Suworow, *Der Tag M*, Klett-Cotta, Stuttgart 1995; V. Suworow, *Stalins verhinderter Erstschlag*, Pour le Merite, Selente 2000; E. Topitsch, *Stalin's War*, Fourth Estate, London 1987; W. Post, *Unternehmen Barbarossa*, Mittler, Hamburg 1995; F. Becker, *Stalins Blutspur durch Europa*, Arndt Verlag, Kiel 1996; F. Becker, *Im Kampf um Europa*, Leopold Stocker Verlag, Graz/Stuttgart 1993; W. Maser, *Der Wortbruch. Hitler, Stalin und der Zweite Weltkrieg*, Olzog Verlag, Munich 1994; J. Hoffmann, *Stalin's War of Extermination*, Theses & Dissertations Press, Capshaw, AL, 2000; J. Hoffmann, *"Die Sowjetunion bis zum Vorabend des deutschen Angriffs"*, in: Horst Boog and others, *Das Deutsche Reich und der Zweite Weltkrieg*, vol. 4: *Der Angriff auf die Sowjetunion*, Deutsche Verlags-Anstalt, Stuttgart 1987; J. Hoffmann, *"The Soviet Union's Offensive Preparations in 1941"*, in: *From Peace to War*. Providence/Oxford, 1997, pp. 361-380.

33 Boris S. Telpuchowski, *Die sowjetische Geschichte des Großen Vaterländischen Krieges 1941-1945*, Frankfurt a. M. 1961, requoted from Walter Sanning, *The Dissolution of the Eastern European Jewry*, Institute for Historical Review, Newport Beach, CA, 1983, p. 104 (online (German): http://vho.org/D/da); cf. Germar Rudolf and Sibylle Schröder, *"Partisanenkrieg und Repressaltötungen"*, *Vierteljahreshefte für freie Geschichtsforschung* (hereafter *VffG*), 3(2) (1999), pp. 145-153 (online: http://vho.org/VffG/ 1999/2/RudolfSchroeder145-153.html).

34 On the question of the legality of such reprisals, cf. Karl Siegert, *"Reprisals and Orders From Higher Up"*, E. Gauss (ed.), *op. cit.* (note 29), pp. 529-548 (online: http://codoh.com/found/fndSiegert.html) and also F.W. Seidler, *Die Wehrmacht im Partisanenkrieg*, Pour le Mérite, Selent 1998; Bogdan Musial, *Konterrevolutionäre Elemente sind zu erschießen*, Propyläen, Berlin 2000.

Because from the very beginning, Jews in the Soviet Union had played an inordinately large role in the making of the Communist system,[35] and also made up a disproportionately large share of the partisans,[36] Jewish civilians suffered in the German repression measures to a much greater degree than non-Jewish civilians. That there were even 'wild' shootings, which is to say, shootings that were done not as a reaction to attacks by partisans, can hardly be excluded. It is also not disputed that many Jewish-Communist commissars were killed because of Hitler's 1941 *"Commissar Order,"* which was only reluctantly applied by German officers in the East and which was abrogated in early 1942. In addition, thousands of Jews were killed in pogroms initiated by the native populations following the German invasion. After they had been freed from the Bolshevist yoke, Latvians, Lithuanians, Ukrainians and others took revenge on Jews because the Red terror machinery had been led mainly by Jews, and this retribution unfortunately fell also on Jews who had nothing to do with the Communist crimes.[37]

The orthodox historians are telling us that the Germans carried out an actual war of extermination against the Jews. The most extensive presentation of this thesis was the book published in 1981 by Helmut Krausnick and Hans-Heinrich Wilhelm, *Die Truppe des Weltanschauungskrieges*,[38] which we cannot examine further in a work dedicated solely to the discussion of Hilberg; that will have to wait until a later date. In what follows we will critically examine the arguments Raul Hilberg has made in support of this thesis. First, however, we need to summarize what Hilberg says happened to Soviet Jews in the German-occupied territories.

2. Hilberg's Version of German Jewish Policy in the Occupied Soviet Territories

Raul Hilberg states that the mass murders of Soviet Jews began in August 1941; he writes:

> *"At first the Kommandos undertook no mass shootings nor made victims of whole families. They had not yet become habituated to routine kill-*

---

35 Of 531 leading personalities in the Soviet Union in 1920, 447 were Jews, cf. Juri K. Begunov, *Tajnye Sily w istorii Rossij*, Isdatelstvo Imeni A.S. Syborina, St. Petersburg 1996.

36 *Die Enzyklopädie des Holocaust* (ed. by Eberhard Jäckel, Peter Longerich and Julius H. Schoeps, Argon Verlag, Berlin 1993) contains this comment: *"The partisan groups* [in the USSR] *often formed spontaneously. Many units consisted largely of Jewish fighters."* (p. 1348).

37 All six main architects of the Communist slave camp system were Jews (Alexander Solschenizyn, *Der Archipel Gulag*, Scherz Verlag, Bern 1974, photographic section).

38 Stuttgart 1981.

ing. Because of the influence of centuries-old traditions they did not consider their orders as all-encompassing. They took the word 'Jew' to mean men only. The mass killings started only in August 1941." (p. 307; *DEJ*, na)

The *"Kommandos"* belonged to the four *Einsatzgruppen*, which had been formed before the war and were intended to secure German rear areas, meaning they were to fight partisans operating behind the lines. According to Hilberg, they had two further responsibilities. Referring to an affidavit made after the war by Otto Ohlendorf, leader of *Einsatzgruppe D*,[39] he writes:

> *"According to Ohlendorf, the commanders of the Einsatzgruppen were briefed by Himmler personally. They were informed that an important part of their task was the elimination* (Beseitigung) *of Jews—women, men and children—and of Communist functionaries.[26]"* (p. 303; *DEJ*, p. 290)

Also, Hilberg says, the *Einsatzgruppen* were to comb the POW camps for persons they should shoot. Heydrich had ordered the sorting out of all *"professional revolutionaries"*, Red Army political officers, *"fanatical Communists"* and *"all Jews"*, and the *Einsatzgruppen* did the major part of this work (p. 351; *DEJ*, p. 335).

The four *Einsatzgruppen* numbered 3,000 men altogether, including a few noncombatants, such as interpreters and radio operators (pp. 302f.; *DEJ*, p. 289).

The first *"killing sweep"*, which began in August 1941, lasted until December of the same year, but before it was over a second killing sweep had already begun—in the fall—, whose purpose was the seizure and liquidation of Jews who had been overlooked.

In addition to the *Einsatzgruppen*, *Gestapo* members from Tilsit, *Einsatzkommandos* from the Generalgouvernement and improvised *Kommandos* of the Higher SS and Police Leaders cooperated in the second killing sweep. (p. 312; *DEJ*, p. 298).

The mass shootings followed the same pattern, apart from minor variations: Jews would be taken from the cities where most of them lived to pits lying on the outskirts of the cities—some of which already existed, the rest of which were dug for the purpose—and murdered there. Frequently there were five or six layers of bodies in the pits before they were covered over with earth. (pp. 333f.; *DEJ*, p. 318f.).

Because the shootings often caused stressful misgivings for the shooters, Hilberg tells us the Germans instituted the use of gas vans as

---

39 PS-3710.

another instrument of murder starting in December 1941, when each *Einsatzgruppe* was allotted two or three of them. Jews were killed in the gas vans with exhaust gas fed inside (pp. 349f.; *DEJ*, na).

Here are the victim counts Hilberg gives for several cities:

- 33,000 victims in Kiev;
- 10,600 victims in Riga (this *Einsatzkommando* numbered only 21 men!);
- 23,600 victims in Kamenets-Podolsk;
- 15,000 victims in Dnepropetrovsk (p. 311; *DEJ*, p. 298);
- 15,000 victims in Rovno (p. 312; *DEJ*, p. 298);
- 10,000 victims in Simferopol (p. 391; *DEJ*, p. 373).

Hilberg charges large-scale massacres of Jews not only to the Germans, but also to the Rumanians, who he claims slaughtered 19,000 Jews in a single day, 23rd October 1941 (p. 321; *DEJ*, p. 306).

Although the second killing sweep allegedly got under way a full three months before the first had ended, Hilberg says that there was an *"intermediary stage"*, that of ghettoization. Its purposes were twofold. Referring to a (supposed) report of *Einsatzgruppe C*, he writes:

> *"All Einsatzgruppen commanders, with the possible exception of the relentless Dr. Stahlecker,* [the leader of Einsatzgruppe A] *realized that the Jews could not be killed in a single sweep. In one report there is even a note of despair over the Jewish refugees who were drifting back into the cities from which they had fled. [...] Whenever the Einsatzgruppe had left a town, it returned to find more Jews than had already been killed there.[2]"* (p. 358; *DEJ*, p. 342)

The essence of the ghettos, Hilberg believes, was to:

> *"prevent the dispersal of the victims and to facilitate their future seizure for shootings."* (p. 366; *DEJ*, p. 349)

The second purpose motivating ghettoization was the economic utilization of Jews:

> *"Whereas the mobile killing units were interested only in concentrating the Jews to facilitate the second sweep, the military and civilian administrations decided to exploit the situation while it lasted. Hence economic measures, in the form of labor utilization and property confiscations, became an important aspect of the intermediary stage."* (p. 372; *DEJ*, p. 355)

> *"The army needed Jewish workers in its repair shops and Jewish clerks in its offices.[60] The armament plants under 'trusteeship' continued to be dependent upon Jewish labor.[61] In the Volhynian sector of the Generalkommissariat Volhynia-Podolia, the labor force in armament plants was 90 percent Jewish throughout 1941 and 1942.[62]"* (p. 376; *DEJ*, p. 359)

Although the ghettoization policy as an *"intermediary stage"* occurred between the first killing sweep—completed by December 1941—and the second sweep beginning in September 1941,

> *"When the civil administration took over part of the occupied territory in July and August of 1941, the mobile killing units had already completed a large part of the ghettoization process. Einsatzgruppe A prided itself that, upon transfer of jurisdiction, it had already made preparations for the incarceration in ghettos of all Jewish communities (excepting only Vilna).[9]"* (p. 361; *DEJ*, pp. 344f.)

The ghettos of Riga and Minsk were also designated for the reception of deported German Jews. But since the available space did not suffice for both the local Jews and the German Jews together, in Riga between the 29th November and the 9th December 1941 the National Socialists shot 27,800 Jews in two sweeps (after they had already butchered 10,600 there earlier). *"Space had now been created for transports from Germany inside the ghetto itself."* (p. 370; *DEJ*, p. 353). Yet the German Jews in the Riga quarter and in the nearby work camps were reduced to a handful of survivors in the months and years following their deportation at the end of 1941, due to the depredations of unchecked epidemics (p. 371; *DEJ*, p. 353). This caused the Germans much harm economically, because:

> *"In the Riga region, where the German Jews were to be 'quartered only for a transitory stay (*nur vorübergehend hier untergebracht)*', and where many of the deportees were 'cripples, war invalids, and people over seventy years of age (*Krüppel, Kriegsinvaliden und über 70 Jahre alte Leute)[65], a widespread demand for Jewish laborers became manifest all the same. On one occasion a Gebietskommissar employee complained that soldiers, shouting in the presence of more than 1,000 Jews, had simply seized the labor in defiance of regulations.[66] By 1943 the remaining thousands of German and Latvian Jewish laborers were divided among a large number of employers: SS, army, navy, air force, railroads and firms.[67]"* (p. 377; *DEJ*, pp. 359f.)

From the transports reaching Minsk from Germany and the Protectorate of Bohemia and Moravia, 5,000 Jews were shot on the 25th and 29th November (p. 371; *DEJ*, p. 353).

Around the middle of 1943, Heinrich Himmler decided to liquidate the entire ghetto system; the ghettos would be converted into concentration camps. This conversion was completed smoothly in Latvia, but in Lithuania it was accompanied by extensive killing operations (p. 407; *DEJ*, p. 388). Hilberg reports:

> *"By August and September 1943, the Vilna ghetto was dissolved. Most of its inmates were sent to Estonia and Latvia, where they were subjected to attrition and shootings, and from where the remainder was subse-*

quently routed to the Stutthof concentration camp. Other thousands were transported to the Lublin death camp, and still others were rounded up and shot." (p. 405; *DEJ*, p. 385)

Jews in the Minsk ghetto were removed to Poland (p. 407; *DEJ*, p. 388).

All told, according to Hilberg, 1.35 million Jews perished in the Soviet territories taken by the Germans. Of these, more than two thirds were murdered by the *Einsatzgruppen*; the rest were killed by troops of the Higher SS and Police Leaders, of the Wehrmacht and the Rumanians, fell in partisan warfare or died due to privations in the camps and ghettos and in the open fields and woods (pp. 409f.; *DEJ*, p. 390). A further 1.5 million Soviet Jews escaped German rule through flight (p. 305; *DEJ*, p. 291). Since, of the five million Jews living in the USSR before 22nd June 1941, four million were inhabitants of zones which at times came under German control, under these conditions over one million Jews must have survived in the area ruled by the Germans (pp. 304f.; *DEJ*, p. 291).

Now, this is Hilberg's description of what happened to the Jews in the Soviet territories overrun by the Germans. Before we take a look at the sources on which the exalted 'Holocaust' historian founds his assertions, let us pursue the question whether the picture he draws appears believable or not, using good common sense.

3. On the Likelihood of Hilberg's Description

Anyone endowed with the power of logical thought who analyzes Hilberg's description of German Jewish policy in the occupied Soviet territories as summarized above will inescapably come to the conclusion that it cannot hold up, and consequently it must rest on unreliable sources. Let us list some of the more gross absurdities which spring into view:

a. The Claimed Numbers of Victims of the *Einsatzgruppen*

The claimed numbers of victims of the *Einsatzgruppen* are impossibly large. The largest of the four, *Einsatzgruppe A*, had 990 members. If we subtract from this the 172 vehicle drivers, 3 women employees, 51 interpreters, 3 teletypewriter operators and 8 radio operators, there are about 750 combatants left to use for the mass killings (p. 303; *DEJ*, p. 289). Up to 15th October 1941, *Einsatzgruppe A* supposedly killed 125,000 Jews (p. 309; *DEJ*, p. 289). Considering the fact that the mass murders first began in August (p. 307; *DEJ*, na), the overwhelming majority of the 125,000 victims, let us say 120,000, must have been killed in a period of ten weeks.

Since the Jews certainly cannot have gone to their deaths willingly, they must have been tracked down and driven together in the cities, where there certainly would have been escape attempts and resistance. Also there would have been the difficulty of moving the condemned to the outskirts of the city, where most of the pits undoubtedly would have had to have been newly dug.

Besides carrying out the massacres, the *Einsatzgruppen* were required to comb the POW camps for commissars, fanatical Communists and Jews. This would have been an immense task, because, up to the end of 1941, no less than 3,350,000 Red Army members had fallen into German hands (p. 351; *DEJ*, p. 334). Even when one considers that only a part of them had been captured by the middle of October, that the *Einsatzgruppen* did not have to do all the work, only *"the major part"* of it, and that there were four *Einsatzgruppen*, under these conditions, during the ten weeks from the beginning of August until the middle of October *Einsatzgruppe A* must have searched through hundreds of thousands of POWs for the persons to be liquidated—in addition to shooting 120,000 Jews and fighting partisans!

One example is sufficient. In view of Hilberg's strong tendency to exaggerate, we will not go into the astronomical number of victims Hilberg attributes to the other *Einsatzgruppen*.

b. The Refugees Drifting back into the Cities

It is pure flimflam to say that *"the Jewish refugees [...] were drifting back into the cities from which they had fled"*, which meant that whenever the *Einsatzgruppe* had left a town, it returned to find more Jews than had already been killed there (p. 358; *DEJ*, p. 342). If it is really true that significant numbers of Jews returned to the cities captured by the Germans, is this not an infallible indication that the Germans *did not* massacre the Jews, since word of such a thing would have spread like wildfire. Killing operations of this magnitude are not easy to hide, especially when they supposedly took place near a city, as in the case of Babi Yar.

c. The Purpose and the Course of the Ghettoization

What Hilberg has written on the subject of ghettoization, its time frame and purpose, defies all logic. We recapitulate:

- The ghettoization occurred between the first killing sweep (terminating at the end of December 1941) and the second (beginning in September 1941), which means it must have been carried out in the last four months of 1941.

41

- In July and August, the *Einsatzgruppen* had already "*completed a large part*" of the ghettoization process.
- The purpose of the ghettoization was partly to facilitate the later seizure of the Jews to shoot them, since "*the Jews could not be killed in a single sweep*".
- The ghettos also allowed Jewish labor forces to be exploited.

This is all a hopeless confusion. *Either* in the East the Germans carried on an extermination policy with respect to the Jews—dictated by ideological fanaticism—*or* they pursued a policy of ghettoization—driven by security considerations as well as economic considerations. The two simply cannot be combined. That ghettoization would not exclude the killing of *certain categories of Jews* (commissars, partisans, hostages and so on) nor would it exclude spontaneous massacres ordered by local commanders, is another question.

Hilberg's argument which he uses to explain the ghettoization, that so many Jews drifted back into the cities captured by the Germans that they could not be killed in a single sweep, is pure nonsense. Why not, when in the first of two massacres in Riga 10,600 Jews could be murdered by 21 men?

Furthermore, if the ghettoization took place sometime between the fall and the end of 1941, the *Einsatzgruppen* can hardly have already "*completed a large part*" of it as early as July and August!

We move on. In summer 1943, Himmler ordered the conversion of the ghettos to concentration camps (why exactly, when their purpose in the first place had been to facilitate shooting the Jews?). In Latvia this happened smoothly, but in Lithuania it required use of force. Were the Lithuanian Jews shot then? Partially yes, Hilberg believes, but not right where they were found, but rather… *in Latvia and Estonia*! Why not in Lithuania itself? The survivors from Latvia and Estonia were sent to *Sobibór* in East Poland, a place Hilberg says was an 'extermination camp' used only for gassing Jews, so that the purpose of sending them there can only have been to kill them.

Why these Lithuanian Jews would not have been killed in Latvia and Estonia, instead of once more having valuable transport space and food thrown away on them, remains a mystery. And how did some of these Lithuanian Jews sent to Latvia and Estonia end up in the camp at *Stutthof*, lying east of Danzig, which Hilberg says was *not* a extermination camp?[40]

Let us move on to the German and Czech Jews, who were removed to Riga and Minsk at the end of 1941.

If, as Hilberg says, the Hitler order for the physical annihilation of Jewry had been given long before, the purpose of these measures can only have been the killing of the deportees. (We repeat here the question raised before, why the Germans would not have just killed them on the spot, or at least have waited another month until the opening of the first 'extermination camp' at Chełmno.) In fact, says Hilberg, 5,000 of the Jews from the Reich and the Protectorate who reached Minsk were killed immediately on arrival. The rest of them were later sent backward *to Poland*, although whether to be killed or to work there, Hilberg does not say. In Riga, many of the unfortunate people died, too, but not by shooting, but because of raging epidemics. This meant a significant economic loss to the Germans, since the survivors performed valuable work for the "*SS, army, navy, air force, railway service and manufacturing concerns*". Wouldn't the Germans had done better, if they had not murdered the 27,800 Latvian Jews who were allegedly shot to make room for the German Jews, not to mention the 10,600 already killed by the 21 men?

"*It was dark and the moon shone brightly as a speeding motor car slowly turned around the straight corner. Within were seated standing people, silently sunk in conversation…*" This is the beginning of a well-known German non-sense nursery rhyme. Hilberg's rendition of German policy on the Jews in the conquered Soviet territories sounds exactly like it.

4. No Valid Evidence for the Claimed Approximately 1.2 Million Murdered Jews Behind the Eastern Front

In the beginning of 1943 the Germans found a mass grave containing 4,000 victims at Katyn in White Russia. They soon discovered that the victims had been some of the Polish officers and soldiers who had been taken prisoner by the Soviets in 1939. A quickly convened international expert commission confirmed this evaluation. The National Socialists used this grisly discovery for an immense and very successful anti-Bolshevist propaganda campaign. In Nuremberg, the Soviets succeeded in putting the guilt on the Germans, but no one in Poland or the West really believed them. It was not until Mikhail Gorbachev in 1990 that Moscow confessed that these Polish fighters had been shot by Stalin's thugs—along with more than 10,000 others buried in other locations.[41]

---

40 Even today in Poland, it is asserted that there were gassings of persons in Stutthof; the visitor is shown a disinfestation chamber opposite the crematory as the crime site. Yet Western historians have mostly kept away from this subject. Hilberg never mentions gassings of persons in Stutthof, which shows that he does not regard that camp as an 'extermination camp'; cf. on this Jürgen Graf, Carlo Mattogno, *Concentration Camp Stutthof*, Theses & Dissertations Press, Capshaw, AL, 2001.

41 On the Katyn massacre see, for example, Allen Paul, *Katyn, The Untold Story of Stalin's Polish Massacre*, Charles Scribner's Sons, New York [2]1991.

Raul Hilberg's version is that, of the original 4 million Jews in the German occupied territories of the USSR, approximately 1.35 millions died, and only a small number of them in ghettos, camps or in the partisan war; most of them were murdered. If we take *"most of them"* to mean an even 1.2 million, this means that the Germans in the USSR killed almost three hundred times as many Jews as the Soviets had killed Polish fighters at Katyn. Undoubtedly, the Communists would not have let slip this unique opportunity to repay their adversary the shame of Katyn with interest and compounded interest! Undoubtedly, as the Germans had done previously, the Soviets would have flown in international expert commissions such as the International Committee of the Red Cross. Undoubtedly, at the Nuremberg trials they would have shown films of the exhumation of hundreds of thousands of murdered Jews!

Nothing of the sort happened. Raul Hilberg explains why:

> *"In June 1942, Himmler ordered the commander of Sonderkommando 4a, Standartenführer Paul Blobel, 'to erase the traces of Einsatzgruppen executions in the East'. Blobel formed a special Kommando with the code designation 1005. The Kommando had the task of digging up graves and burning bodies. Blobel traveled all over the occupied territories, looking for graves and conferring with Security Police officials. Once he took a visitor from the RSHA* [Reichssicherheitshauptamt] *(Hartl) for a ride and, like a guide showing historical places to a tourist, pointed to the mass graves near Kiev, where his own men had killed 34,000 Jews.[93]*
>
> *From the beginning, however, Blobel had to contend with problems. [...] When the Russians overran the occupied territories, Blobel had fulfilled only part of his task.[96]"* (pp. 408f.; *DEJ*, p. 389)

As his source for these statements, Hilberg gives not a document from the period itself, but instead Blobel's affidavit made for one of the Nuremberg successor trials.[42]

If Blobel could accomplish *"only part"* of his task, then the Soviets must have found numerous unopened mass graves. The reason they did not fully exploit this discovery is unclear.

Let us assume that *"only part"* means that Blobel was able to open and incinerate the corpses in half the graves, i.e., 600,000 corpses. As fuel, we are told, he chose not wood, which would have been easy to come by in those heavily wooded areas, but gasoline! If one were to pour gasoline on a corpse lying in the open and set it on fire, most of the gasoline would seep into the ground. To prevent this one would have to lay the cadaver in a container—such as a metal tub; in this case, one would need about 16 gallons

---

42 NO-3947.

per incineration.[43] The gasoline loss would also be less if one lay the corpse on a pile of wood.

Under the unrealistic assumption that Blobel and his people were in possession of the equipment necessary to at least partially prevent the costly gasoline from seeping away, for the incineration of 600,000 corpses they would have needed (600,000 × 16 =) 9,600,000 gallons of gasoline—and this at a time when the scarcity of fuel for airplanes, armored vehicles and trucks was causing the Germans severe difficulties!

With open air incineration using gasoline, bones remain behind, and usually not only splinters, but large pieces of shoulder and pelvic bones. Teeth cannot be destroyed this way at all. Also, a corpse leaves behind ashes, amounting to about 5% of body weight.[44] If, for example, Blobel and his men had wanted to dispose without a trace of the 27,800 Jews Hilberg says were murdered in Riga at the end of 1941, they would have had to do the following:

- They would have had to remove (27,800 × 30 =) 834,000 teeth (we assume that each Jew was missing two teeth, on average).
- They would have had to remove millions of bones.
- They would have had to scatter (27,800 × 2.5 =) 69,500 kilograms of ashes (we assume that each murdered person weighed 50 kg on average, since there would have been many children among them).

With a total of 600,000 corpses to dispose of without a trace, the numbers above increase by a factor of more than twenty. How Blobel and his *Kommando* accomplished this remains a mystery, especially since the murder sites lay in numerous, widely-dispersed localities.

Hilberg never touches on fundamental questions of this kind; he apparently does not even recognize that they pose a problem. As a *"paper historian,"*[45] who avoided any on-site research and forensic investigations, he lives far from the physical reality of things in his world of records and books.

Along with the mass shootings, the Germans are supposed to have killed people in mobile gas vans. As has already been mentioned in our Introduction, Hilberg does not show a single picture of these gas vans. Even the well-known volume *Nationalsozialistische Massentötungen durch Gift-*

---

43 Arnulf Neumaier, *"The Treblinka Holocaust"*; in: Ernst Gauss (ed.), *op. cit.* (note 29) p. 489 (online: http://codoh.com/found/fndtreb.html).

44 *Schlag nach! Natur*, Bibliographisches Institut Leipzig 1952, p. 512, quoted in Arnulf Neumaier, previous footnote.

45 This fitting expression was coined by Robert Faurisson.

gas, which devotes no less than 64 pages to the gas vans, contains no photo-graph.[46] There is a good reason for this: no man has ever laid eyes on one of these legend-shrouded vans.

This is our final result: Hilberg makes no attempt to provide material evidence for the murder of some 1.2 million Jews behind the eastern front.

5. Hilberg's Documentary Evidence

The sources Hilberg cites as proof for murder of the Jews behind the eastern front fall into two broad categories: documents and witness state-ments (the latter includes also confessions of perpetrators, since the perpe-trator is by definition a witness).

We turn first to the documentary evidence. Most of it concerns the so-called "*Operational Reports*" (*Ereignismeldungen*) of the *Einsatzgruppen*, which fall into the time frame June 1941 through May 1942. These are sup-posedly daily reports of the *Einsatzgruppe* commanders to Heinrich Him-mler. Numerous massacres are described in these reports, sometimes with five digit numbers of victims. The Soviets supposedly found these docu-ments in the offices of the *Reichssicherheitshauptamt* in Berlin.

The fact that the Germans would let such incriminating material fall into the hands of their enemies must arouse some surprise. If Germans could bring about the incineration without a trace of several millions of corpses in the 'extermination camps' and behind the eastern front, they would certainly have been able to incinerate a few stacks of paper! Thus, a suspicion of forgery is justified here, right from the start. There are also more technical grounds to dispute the genuineness of the documents, which the American researcher Prof. Arthur R. Butz summarizes as follows:[47]

> "*Besides telling of regular anti-partisan activities, the reports tell of individual actions of mass executions of Jews, with numbers of victims usu-ally running in the thousands. It is indicated, in most cases, that many cop-ies, sometimes as many as a hundred, were distributed.* [Apparently the Germans were intent on letting the rest of the world know as soon as possi-ble about the butchery behind the eastern front!] *They are mimeographed and signatures are most rare and, when they occur, appear on non-incrimi-nating pages. Document NO-3159, for example, has a signature, R.R. Strauch, but only on a covering page giving the locations of various units of the Einsatzgruppen. There is also NO-1128, allegedly from Himmler to Hit-*

---

46 Eugen Kogon, Hermann Langbein, Adalbert Rückerl (eds.), *op. cit.* (note 5). The gas vans are discussed on pages 89 through 146.
47 Arthur Butz, *The Hoax of the Twentieth Century*, Institute for Historical Review, Newport Beach, Calif. 1976, p. 198.

ler reporting, among other things, the execution of 363,211 Russian Jews in August-November 1942. This claim occurs on page 4 of NO-1128, while initials said to be Himmler's occur on the irrelevant page 1. Moreover, Himmler's initials were easy to forge: three vertical lines with a horizontal line drawn through them."

The case of Babi Yar provides an irrefutable proof of the falseness of these Operational Reports. There, on 29th September 1941, shortly after entry into Kiev, as revenge for the operations of the resistance movement which had taken the lives of many members of the Wehrmacht and civilians, the Germans are supposed to have shot 33,000 Jews. The massacre was reported in Operational Report no. 106 of 7th October 1941,[48] in which the number of killed was given with German precision: There were exactly 33,711. The total number of Jews present in Kiev at the time was given by this report as 300,000.

Many more Jews were killed in Babi Yar in the following weeks and months, according to 'Holocaust' writers.

Researchers such as Udo Walendy[49] and Herbert Tiedemann[50] have compiled a long list of inconsistencies which undermine the reality of this supposed mass murder; here are a few of the more important:

- The claimed total numbers of victims diverge wildly and sometimes reach up to 300,000.
- In 1931, approximately 850,000 persons lived in Kiev, of which 140,000 were Jews.[51] After the German invasion of 22nd June 1941, a massive evacuation of the civilian population took place, so that when the Germans arrived, only a little more than 300,000 *Jewish and non-Jewish* inhabitants remained.[52]
- In view of the potential danger to the Jews in a German occupation, the Jewish share of the evacuation must certainly not have been less than average, so that in September 1941 the German army could hardly have encountered more than 45,000 Jews. In these circumstances, Operational Report 106, which mentions 300,000 Jews, seems to be a gross forgery.

---

48 R-102.
49 Udo Walendy, *"Babi Jar – die Schlucht 'mit 33.711 ermordeten Juden'?"*, in: *Historische Tatsachen*, Verlag für Volkstum und Zeitgeschichtsforschung, Vlotho/Weser, no. 51 (1992).
50 Herbert Tiedemann, *"Babi Yar: Critical Questions and Comments"*, in: Ernst Gauss (ed.), *op. cit.* (note 29), pp. 497-525 (online: http://codoh.com/found/fndbabiyar.html); cf. also cf. Germar Rudolf and Sibylle Schröder, *op. cit.* (note 33).
51 *Brockhaus Encyclopädie*, Wiesbaden 1967, quoted from Tiedemann, *op. cit.* (note 50), p. 521.
52 *Zentralblatt des Reichskommissariats für die Ukraine*, Rovno, 2nd year, no. 2, 9th January 1943, pp. 8-20, quoted from Tiedemann (see previous footnote).

- In addition to shooting, some witnesses state that the method of murder used was drowning in the Dnepr, blowing up with mines, blowing up with hand grenades, burial while still alive, squashing with armored vehicles and other such nonsense; today the orthodox historiography is painfully silent about these other methods of killing.

- The witnesses cannot agree on the exact site of the crime any more than on the method of killing.

- The Soviets have never bothered to perform forensic investigations of traces or to preserve traces.

- After the war, the supposed crime site was used unchanged as a garbage dump (!)—such lack of piety is not to be expected from the Soviets, who have always honored their martyrs.

The definitive proof that the massacre at Babi Yar never took place is given by the German air-reconnaissance photographs of the area, which the specialist John Ball has studied.[53] In September 1943, shortly before the Red Army retook Kiev, the Germans supposedly exhumed and incinerated the bodies, finishing on the 29th September. An air-reconnaissance photograph of 26th September shows that the ravine of Babi Yar was free of any human activity at that time. No groups of people, no vehicles, no piles of firewood, no fire and no smoke are evident. Neither the topography nor the vegetation— except for the natural growth of the trees—had changed as compared to 1941.

That unmasks the mass shooting at Babi Yar as a propaganda lie, and the fact that it surfaces in an Operational Report means that any reports of the *Einsatzgruppen* must be considered suspect in advance and subject to a careful expert analysis.

No other claimed German massacre behind the eastern front was exploited to the extent of that at Babi Yar. The main 'proof' for this massacre is one of the Operational Reports. How credible, then, are other mass murders, likewise 'proven' by Operational Reports?

Of course it is possible—even likely—that genuine reports of the *Einsatzgruppen* fell into the hands of the Soviets. If it did happen, the real reports could have served as examples for forgeries in which either the numbers of victims of real massacres was enlarged or massacres which never happened were invented.

---

53 John C. Ball, *"Air Photo Evidence"*; in: E. Gauss (ed.), *op. cit.* (note 29), p. 275f. (online: http:// www.air-photo.com, http://codoh.com/found/fndaerial.html).

A few more words on the gas vans, which Hilberg mentions only briefly (pp. 349f.; *DEJ*, pp. 333f.). The only documentary proof he cites for their existence is the letter supposedly written by SS-Untersturmführer Becker to SS-Obersturmführer Walter Rauff on 16th May 1942.[54]

Ingrid Weckert has pointed out that this document is probably a forgery.[55] On the basis of a comprehensive study of all the evidence in existence pertaining to this subject, Pierre Marais has demonstrated that goods trucks mentioned therein could not have served as "*gas vans*". For one thing, the original specifications of the manufacturer of these goods trucks show that the cargo space was only 1.50 m high (4ft 11in).[56]

The technical ineptness of the gas van story comes from the fact that these murder vehicles were supposed to have been Saurer 5 tonners (p. 349; *DEJ*, na). All Saurer vehicles were powered with Diesel engines, but the exhaust gases of Diesel engines are poorly suited to killing due to their high oxygen and very low CO content. The same Saurer firm which manufactured those vans who are most likely mislabeled as "*gas vans*," also produced massive numbers of goods vehicles fueled by generator gas. This gas was generated by burning moist wood and coke with a restricted amount of oxygen. Since this fuel replaces gasoline, it was used by the hundreds of thousands in Germany during the Second World War. Generator gas has a CO content of up to 35%, which is quickly fatal. Thus, in contrary to Diesel exhaust gases, these gas generators themselves would have been ideal murder instruments. But there is no report on their use for mass killing.[57]

6. Hilberg's 'Affidavits' and Other Witness Evidence

Many of the charges that have been made against the Third Reich based on witness statements have long since been retracted by the orthodox historians. For example, no one asserts any longer that the Germans have the massacre of Katyn on their conscience, although this charge was made to stick at the Nuremberg Tribunal.[58] The horror story about soap from human fat[59]—likewise dished out by the Soviets at Nuremberg—is not

---

54 PS-501.
55 Ingrid Weckert, "*The Gas Vans: A Critical Assessment of the Evidence*"; in: Ernst Gauss (ed.), *op. cit.* (note 29), pp. 217-243 (online: http://codoh.com/found/fndwagon.html).
56 Pierre Marais, *Les camions à gaz en question*, Polémiques, Paris 1994, especially pp. 135-141.
57 Friedrich Paul Berg, "*The Diesel Gas Chambers: Ideal for Torture—Absurd for Murder*"; in: E. Gauss (ed.), *op. cit.* (note 29), pp. 435-465 (online: http://codoh.com/found/fndieselgc.html). Diesel engines can run both with Diesel fuel and with generator gas.
58 IMT VII, p. 469.
59 IMT VII, pp. 656f.

taken seriously by any reputable historian; even Hilberg describes it as a *"rumor"* (pp. 1032f.; *DEJ*, p. 967). Other accusations which the Soviet prosecutors made against Germany at Nuremberg have been long forgotten and apparently sprang from more twisted minds than the soap fairy tale.

For example, the Soviets accused the National Socialists of having murdered 840,000 Russian POWs in concentration camp Sachsenhausen by means of pedal-driven skull smashing machines.[60]

The Western Allies did not lag behind the Soviets in their clumsy horror propaganda. Thus at the Nuremberg trial, US prosecutor Robert Jackson falsely denounced the Germans to former German armaments minister Albert Speer for having blown up 20,000 Jews with an atom bomb at Auschwitz.[61] The number of dead at Dachau was for years posted on a signboard on the grounds of the former concentration camp as 238,000, while the actual number was approximately 30,000, of which it is now undisputed that at least half died in the last four months of the war when the transport system had collapsed and epidemics spread unchecked.[62]

Also at Nuremberg the Anglo-Americans paid obeisance to the lies about gas chamber murders in Dachau, Buchenwald and other western camps. For example, British chief prosecutor Sir Hartley Shawcross asserted there that the Germans had "*conducted* [murder] *like some mass production industry in the gas chambers and the ovens of Auschwitz, Dachau, Treblinka, Buchenwald, Mauthausen, Maidanek, and Oranienburg.*".[63] These things so embarrass present-day 'Holocaust' historians that they prefer not to denounce them as terrible lies, in most cases they do not even dare to mention them.

An interesting collection of nonsense accusations thrown around at the Nuremberg trial has been assembled by Carlos Porter and Vincent Reynouard.[64]

All these invented German atrocities were confirmed by 'eye-witness reports' and 'perpetrator confessions' whose value is difficult to assess. The same applies to the numerous witness statements about massacres behind the eastern front, a substantial proportion of which were furnished for the Nuremberg trial or its successor trials. One example is the aforementioned affidavit of Paul Blobel on his activities behind the eastern front. Blobel deposed that he and his *Kommando 1005* had exhumed a large part of the

---

60   IMT VII, pp. 416f.
61   IMT XVI, pp. 579f.
62   Paul Berben, *Dachau. The Official History*, The Norfolk Press, 1975.
63   IMT XIX, p. 434.
64   Carlos Porter and Vincent Reynouard, *Menteur à Nuremberg*, ANEC, BP 21, F-44530, 1998.

mass graves and incinerated the bodies of the murdered victims. At the same time, according to another affidavit, that of an RSHA man named Hartl, *"like a guide showing historical places to a tourist,* [Blobel] *pointed to the mass graves near Kiev, where his own men had killed 34,000 Jews"*.[65] Since this massacre near Kiev (Babi Yar) cannot have taken place, the affidavit is necessarily fraudulent.

The victorious powers did not lack the means to compel such witness testimony. In 1948 a US delegation led by judges Gordon Simpson and Edward van Roden determined that the Americans had regularly resorted to torture to procure confessions.[66] In other cases the accused were persuaded to incriminate themselves or their fellow accused by promises of acquittal or light punishment. Wilhelm Höttl is a notable example.[67] If the 'democratic' Americans resorted to such methods, it is hardly likely that the Soviets were any more honorable in their methods.

This is the nature of the 'eye-witness reports' and 'perpetrator confessions' that Raul Hilberg adduces as evidence for the genocide against the Soviet Jews. What follows is a quotation from one such witness statement, which we give as a drastic demonstration of what the world-famous 'Holocaust' Giant foists upon his readers. The passage in question is given on pages 347 and 348 (*DEJ*, pages 332 and 333); Hilberg's source is an article that appeared in the German language US Jewish newspaper *Aufbau* (New York) on 23rd August 1946, which was based on a statement attributed to SS-Obergruppenführer Erich von dem Bach-Zelewski. Hilberg does not tell the reader when and where the confession was supposedly made.

> *"Once, in mid-August 1941, Himmler himself visited Minsk. He asked Einsatzgruppe B Commander* [Arthur] *Nebe to shoot a batch of a hundred people, so that he could see what one of these 'liquidations' really looked like. Nebe obliged. All except two of the victims were men. Himmler spotted in the group a youth of about twenty who had blue eyes and blond hair. Just before the firing was to begin, Himmler walked up to the doomed man and put a few questions to him.*
>
> > *Are you a Jew?*
> > *Yes.*
> > *Are both of your parents Jews?*
> > *Yes.*
> > *Do you have any ancestors who were not Jews?*
> > *No.*
> > *Then I can't help you!*

---

65 NO-5384, mentioned by Hilberg on p. 408 (*DEJ*, p. 389).
66 Arthur R. Butz, *op. cit.* (note 47), p. 24.
67 Germar Rudolf, *op. cit.* (note 29), p. 183f.

> As the firing started, Himmler was even more nervous. During every volley he looked to the ground. When the two women could not die, Himmler yelled to the police sergeant not to torture them.
>
> When the shooting was over, Himmler and a fellow spectator engaged in conversation. The other witness was Obergruppenführer von dem Bach-Zelewski, the same man who was later delivered to a hospital. Von dem Bach addressed Himmler:
>
> > Reichsführer, those were only a hundred.
> > What do you mean by that?
> > Look at the eyes of the men in this Kommando, how deeply shaken they are! These men are finished for the rest of their lives. What kind of followers are we training here? Either neurotics or savages!
>
> Himmler was visibly moved and decided to make a speech to all who were assembled there. He pointed out that the Einsatzgruppe were called upon to fulfill a repulsive (widerliche) duty. He would not like it if Germans did such a thing gladly. But their conscience was in no way impaired, for they were soldiers who had to carry out every order unconditionally. He alone had responsibility before God and Hitler for everything that was happening. […]
>
> After the speech Himmler, Nebe, von dem Bach, and the chief of Himmler's Personal Staff, [Karl] Wolff, inspected an insane asylum. Himmler ordered Nebe to end the suffering of these people as soon as possible. At the same time, Himmler asked Nebe 'to turn over in his mind' various other killing methods more humane than shooting. Nebe asked for permission to try out dynamite on the mentally ill people. Von dem Bach and Wolff protested that the sick people were not guinea pigs, but Himmler decided in favor of the attempt. Much later, Nebe confided to von dem Bach that the dynamite had been tried on the inmates with woeful results.[179]"

Who would have ever thought it? *Einsatzgruppe* commander Arthur Nebe, once a chief of criminal police in civilian life, then a technical bungler who wanted to practice mass murder with explosives!

Hilberg treats 'eye-witness reports' and 'perpetrator confessions' such as these as though they had the same evidentiary value as indisputably authentic documents!

7. Hilberg's Invented 'Shooting of Baltic Camp Inmates'

Concerning the deportation of Jews from the Baltic states to Reich German camps, Hilberg writes that the Baltic camps had been broken up a few months after May 1944:

> "From August 1944 to January 1945, several thousand Jews were transported to concentration camps in the Reich. Many thousands of Baltic camp inmates were shot on the spot, just before the arrival of the Red Army.[90]" (p. 408; *DEJ*, p. 388)

The "*concentration camps in the Reich*" were concentration camp Stutthof (mentioned by Hilberg on p. 405; *DEJ*, p. 385), as well as Kaufering, an outlying camp of Dachau (not mentioned by Hilberg).[68]

Study of the sources for concentration camp Stutthof reveals the following facts:

Between the 12th July and the 14th October 1944 10,458 Jews were transferred to Stutthof from Kaunas (Lithuania) and 14,585 Jews were transferred there from Riga (Latvia); here are the dates and the loading of the respective transports.[69]

DATE	ORIGIN	NUMBER TRANSFERRED
12.7.	Kaunas	282
13.7.	Kaunas	3,098
13.7.	Kaunas	233
16.7.	Kaunas	1,172
17.7.	Kaunas	1,208
19.7.	Kaunas	1,097
19.7.	Kaunas	1,072
25.7.	Kaunas	182
25.7.	Kaunas	1,321
4.8.	Kaunas	793
9.8.	Riga	6,382
9.8.	Riga	450
23.8.	Riga	2,079
23.8.	Riga	2,329
1.10.	Riga	3,155
14.10.	Riga	190
TOTAL:		25,043

If Stutthof alone received 25,043 Jews from the Baltic states and additionally a number of Baltic Jews—unknown to us—were sent to the Dachau outlying camp Kaufering, the total number of Jews divided among concentration camps in Reich territory cannot have been merely a "*few thousand*", as Hilberg states. The reason for this impudent manipulation of numbers is not hard to understand: Hilberg wants to count the 'missing' Jews from the Baltic camps as victims of German mass shootings.

---

68 E. Jäckel, P. Longerich, J.H. Schoeps (ed.), *op. cit.* (note 36), v. II, p. 806.
69 Archiwum Muzeum Stutthof, I-IIB-8, p. 1.

This trickery is all the more culpable inasmuch as the transfers from Kaunas and Riga to Stutthof had been ably documented by Polish historian Krzysztof Dunin-Wąsowicz in 1967.[70]

There can be little excuse for an academic historian who has set himself the high task of producing a *"definitive"* work on the 'Holocaust' who lacks knowledge of the pertinent literature or of the Polish language.

Naturally, as 'proof' of the shooting of Baltic-Jewish camp inmates, Hilberg offers no document, only a witness statement; that of a certain Jew Joseph Tenenbaum.

8. What Really Happened to the Jews in the Occupied Soviet Territories?

In view of the catastrophic lack of documentation, under the present circumstances it is an impossible task to give the number of Soviet Jews killed by the Germans even approximately. The question is incomparably more difficult than, for example, the question of the alleged gassings of persons in Auschwitz. The latter supposedly took place in clearly identified structures described in construction drawings and partially still in existence today, whose suitability for the purpose of mass gassing of persons can be technically evaluated. However, with respect to the—real and claimed—mass shootings behind the eastern front in places mostly unknown, it will not be possible to make an examination of the crime scene after a half century. Only archaeological excavations could help us at this point, if only one knew where in the vastness of Russia one should dig.

We believe that the successor states to the USSR are in possession of German documents which would clarify this aspect of the events behind the eastern front, but that the documents in question are not being made available for political reasons. The question of Jewish population losses in the East cannot be settled until they can be examined. It is also possible that previously unknown air-reconnaissance photographs will be discovered that could shed light on the reality or lack of reality of massacres such as claimed for Babi Yar.

Despite the mass shootings of Soviet Jews that did occur behind the eastern front, everything points to the conclusion that the Germans pursued a general policy of a physical concentration of Jews, and that from early on. One indication of this is a report of the commander of the 350th Infantry Regiment on 19th August 1941, containing this statement:[71]

---

70 Krzysztof Dunin-Wąsowicz, "*Żydowscy Więźniowie KL Stutthof*", in: *Biuletyn Żydowskiego Instytutu Historycznego*, Warsaw 1967, no. 63, p. 10.

"The Jewish question must be solved radically. I propose that all Jews living in the countryside be rounded up and put in guarded collection and labor camps. Suspicious elements should be eliminated."

It is clear that by *"radical solution"* of the Jewish question, the commander did not mean the extermination of the Jews. The handy trick of accusing the author of the report of using of *"code language"* will not work here, because in that case he would not have written of elimination of *"suspicious elements"* (which unquestionably means 'kill'). To distinguish between such suspicious elements and the rest of the Jews would have been useless in that case.

The ghettoization policy that Hilberg describes extensively confirms this hypothesis. It responded to both security considerations (Jews concentrated in ghettos can be policed more easily) and economic necessity: Hilberg himself has emphasized how important the Jews housed in the Riga ghetto were to the Germans as for their manufacturing skills.

The deportation of German and Czech Jews to Minsk and Riga was nothing other than an improvised and chaotic attempt to set in motion the *"final solution of the Jewish question"* by removal to the East. This policy could not be pursued later because of military reverses to the Germans after 1943.

The transports of Lithuanian and White Russian Jews to Latvia, Estonia and Poland only make sense if the Jews were taken to where there was housing and employment for them. Otherwise the transports would have had no logical purpose.

That the population losses of the Jews were far less than those that Hilberg postulates follows from a comparison of Jewish population figures for several Soviet cities before and after the German occupation. In his book *The Final Solution*, which was considered the standard work prior to Hilberg, the British-Jewish historian Gerald Reitlinger gives a few numbers for 1946:[72]

Kiev:	100,000 Jews	Dnepropetrovsk:	50,000 Jews
Odessa:	80,000 Jews	Vinnitsa:	14,000 Jews

Reitlinger's source for these numbers is an article in the Yiddish language Soviet journal *Ainikeit*, the date of whose publication he does not give. He adds:[72]

---

71 Cited by Hilberg on p. 317. Not given in *DEJ*.
72 Gerald Reitlinger, *The Final Solution. The Attempt to Exterminate the Jews of Europe 1939-1945*, Jason Aronson, Northgate, New Jersey 1987, p. 500.

"These figures were recorded at a time when the homeward trek from the deep interior had only begun."

Based on Soviet enumerations carried out over several different years (between 1923 and 1926), Hilberg gives the following numbers for the pre-war populations of these four cities (pp. 305f.; *DEJ*, p. 292):

Kiev:	140,200 Jews	Dnepropetrovsk:	83,900 Jews
Odessa:	153,200 Jews	Vinnitza:	20,200 Jews

According to Hilberg, 40% of the Jews living in German conquered territories were evacuated or escaped the German armies by flight. If the return *"had just begun"* in 1946, as stated in the Soviet-Jewish journal cited by Reitlinger, a far greater proportion of the Jews of these cities had survived than would be indicated by Hilberg's statistic (40% dead). We also point out that Hilberg's figure of 40% evacuated or fled is too low under the circumstances. In his detailed study *The Dissolution of the Eastern European Jewry*, based almost entirely on Jewish and Allied data, Walter N. Sanning arrives at a figure of up to 80%, although it is true that some of his sources are dubious. For example, he quotes David Bergelson, the secretary of the Jewish Anti-fascist Committee, who stated in Moscow in 1942:[73]

> *"The evacuation saved a decisive majority of Jews of the Ukraine, White Russia, Lithuania, and Latvia. According to information from Vitebsk, Riga and other large centers which were conquered by the Fascists, there were few Jews there when the Germans arrived."*

It is quite possible that Bergelson exaggerated the numbers of evacuated persons to put the services of the Soviets in saving the Jews in the best light.[74] The actual percentage of Jews who fled or were evacuated is probably more than Hilberg's 40% and less than Sanning's 80%. Together with the observation that the return movement had just begun in 1946, the pre-war and post-war Jewish population figures for the above four cities contradict the assertion that Soviet Jews in the German occupied territories lost almost two fifths of their population through mass murder, ghettoization and concentration camps. The actual percentage was certainly far lower.

---

73 Gregor Aronson, *Soviet Russia and The Jews*, New York 1949, p. 18; cited by Walter N. Sanning, *op. cit.* (note 33), p. 94.

74 The Soviet rulers did not reward David Bergelson, since he was later caught up in a Stalinist purge and shot.

VI. The Deportations

1. The Initial Situation

Beginning in 1942, Jews from the German Reich and from states occupied or allied with it were sent in massive numbers to concentration camps and ghettos in Polish territory and lesser numbers were sent to concentration camps in the Reich and camps and ghettos in the occupied Soviet territories. The numbers of those displaced is known very accurately for most of the states in question, thanks to the German deportation lists which have been preserved. From Serge Klarsfeld's research, for example, we know that barely 76,000 Jews were deported from France,[75] which corresponds to a fifth of the Jews living in France, most of them holding foreign passports.[76] For Belgium, the Netherlands and other west European states and for the German Reich, the numbers are also largely undisputed. For Hungary, the number of Jewish deportees is generally recognized to be 438,000, and is only questioned by a single reputable scholar, the American Professor Arthur Butz.[77] However, the deportations from Poland, the demographic core area of European Jewry, are very incompletely documented

---

75 In his study *Le Mémorial de la Déportation des Juifs de France* (Beate and Serge Klarsfeld, Paris 1978) Klarsfeld states that the number of deported French Jews was 75,721. The margin of error cannot be more than 1-2%.
76 Thus most Jews who were French nationals were not affected. How does this coincide with the claimed policy of systematic extermination of the Jews?
77 In the chapter *"Hungarian Jews"* of his book *The Hoax of the Twentieth Century*, op. cit. (note 47), Butz defends the theory that the Veesenmayer Dispatches, which have been used to prove that the number of deportees from Hungary was 438,000, are forgeries, and that the number of Jews deported from Hungary was in reality no more than 100,000. One piece of evidence he cites supporting this argument, among others, is a report of the ICRC on its activities in Hungary dating from 1948, in which there is no mention of mass deportations in the spring and early summer of 1944. Although we do not consider Butz' theory to be definitively refuted, we assume the generally recognized numbers of deportations are correct, since these are supported not only by the Veesenmayer Dispatches, but also by documents from neutral states dating from during the war. For a further discussion on the 1944 deportations of Hungarian Jews, see Jürgen Graf, *"What Happened to the Jews Who Were Deported to Auschwitz but Were Not Registered There?"*, The Journal of Historical Review, 19(4) (2000), p. 4-18, and Arthur Butz, *"On the 1944 Deportations of Hungarian Jews"*, The Journal of Historical Review, 19(4) (2000), p. 19-28.

and the numbers given in the official historical writing are very questionable.

Consequently, in the no less than 515 pages (*DEJ*, 470 pages) that Hilberg devotes to the deportations in the second volume of his work, he moves on largely firm documentary ground with respect to the dates and destinations of the deportations as well as the number of those displaced, with the exception of the key country Poland. He turns first to the situation in that part of Europe where the National Socialists were able to carry out their Jewish policy at their discretion, namely, the Reich itself, the Protectorate of Bohemia and Moravia and the Generalgouvernement and then to those countries where they had to pay more or less respect to domestic governments or at least administrations; Hungary is an example of the first, the Netherlands of the second.

These 515 pages demonstrate clearly Hilberg's strategy of puffing up his work with quantities of useless details.

He inundates his reader with an endless flood of information that has no bearing on the subject named in the title of his work, the "*destruction of the European Jews*". He tells us the Minister of Mines in the Croatian Pavelic regime was named Frkovic, that the Minister of Commerce in the Slovakian Tiso regime was Stano, that the Minister of Public Health in the Romanian Antonescu regime was Tomescu and other useless items. He spends no less than seven pages (pp. 428-435; *DEJ*, pp. 410-416) belaboring the "*administrative juggernaut*" of the Reich railways in detail and bores his reader to tears with a pedantic enumeration of the state secretaries for the Reich railways in the Ministry of Commerce.

In order to reach the desired number of pages he mixes in painstakingly collected anecdotes like the following:

> "*On October 3, 1942, the Propaganda Division in Radom reported a disturbing incident that had resulted from the dispatch of a postcard. The Germans published a paper in Poland, the* Krakauer Zeitung, *for the local German population. The chief of the Radom branch of the paper had received from Lwów a postcard that began (in German): 'I don't know German. You can translate everything from Polish into German.' The card then continued in Polish:*
>
>> You old whore and you old son of a whore Richard (In the German translation: Alte Hurenmetze und du alter Hurenbock Richard). A child has been born to you. May your child suffer throughout his life, as we Jews have suffered because of you. I wish you that from the bottom of my heart.
>
>> *This anonymous note actually disturbed its recipient and worried the propaganda experts. The Propaganda Division feared that it was the beginning of a flood of postcards, and the card was transmitted to the Security Police for tracing.*" (p. 548; *DEJ*, p. 522)

Obviously, passages like this make Hilberg's work thicker, but not better!

2. The Purpose of the Deportations: Labor Deployment versus Extermination

As the war continued, the labor shortage in the German Reich and in the countries under its sway took more and more dramatic forms. An immense quantity of documents testify as to how desperately the National Socialists constantly sought to recruit new workers for their industries—especially their war industries. The deployment of Jewish labor forces played a critical role here. In addition to the Jewish workers living in relative freedom—inhabitants of the Łódź ghetto, for example, who manufactured steel helmets for the Wehrmacht—hundreds of thousands of Jews were sent to concentration camps and labor camps as forced labor or were forced to work in the armaments industry.

Since, as Hilberg says, the Germans pursued a policy of systematic extermination of the Jews, for him the deportations can logically have had only one purpose, to transport the deportees to this very extermination. Now there is considerable documentary evidence for shockingly high death rates in camps and ghettos caused by typhus and other epidemics and also by lack of nutrition, but none for a German goal of extermination and, in particular, none for the presence of 'extermination camps' in which Jews were murdered with gas. On the other hand, many documents demonstrate the deployment of Jews in the war economy. Here are a few examples:

On 25th January 1942, five days after the Wannsee Conference, Heinrich Himmler wrote to the General Inspector of Concentration Camps, Richard Glücks:[78]

> *"Arrange for the induction of 100,000 male Jews and up to 50,000 female Jews into the concentration camps. The concentration camps will be asked to perform great economic tasks in the next few weeks. SS-Gruppenführer Pohl[79] will give you further details."*

On 30th April 1942, at a time when—according to the official version of history—a hundred thousandfold mass extermination was under way in Chełmno and Bełżec and the same thing was about to start in two further 'extermination camps', Sobibór and Auschwitz, Oswald Pohl wrote Himmler a note saying:[80]

---

78 NO-500.
79 Oswald Pohl was director of the WVHA (Wirtschaftsverwaltungshauptamt) of the SS.
80 R-129.

"The war has brought a visible change in the structure of the concentration camps and has fundamentally changed their responsibilities with respect to the deployment of prisoners. The influx of prisoners due to security, reeducation or preventive reasons alone no longer stands in the foreground. The main focus has moved to the economic side. The mobilization of all prisoner labor forces, first for war purposes (armaments industries) and later for peacetime purposes now moves to the foreground.

Necessary measures follow from this realization which require the gradual conversion of the concentration camps from their earlier one-sided political form to an organization conforming to the economic requirements."

On 21st August 1942, a month after Hilberg and other 'Holocaust' giants tell us Treblinka was put in operation as a fifth 'extermination camp', Martin Luther, Chief of the German Section of the Foreign Office, wrote in a memorandum:[81]

"The fundamental principle of German Jewish policy after taking power consisted in furthering Jewish emigration by all possible means. The present war gives Germany the opportunity and the duty to resolve the Jewish question in Europe. [...] Based on the above-mentioned Führer instruction [a Hitler decision taken in August 1940 to remove all Jews from Europe] *the evacuation of Jews out of Germany was begun. It was advisable as soon as possible to get hold of the Jewish nationals of countries who had likewise taken measures with respect to the Jews. [...] The number of Jews removed to the East in this way did not suffice to meet the requirements for labor forces there."*

This sets down point blank that the removal of Jews to the East was for the purpose of utilization of their labor power.

The extremely high death rates in the camps, caused mostly by epidemics, but also by poor nourishment and poor clothing, naturally detracted heavily from their economic usefulness. For this reason, on 28th December 1942 Glücks sent a general notice to all concentration camp commanders in which he held them personally responsible for the conservation of their prisoner labor forces. He wrote:[82]

"The senior camp medical doctors will use all the means at their disposal to insure that mortality rates in the several camps decrease substantially. [...] The camp medical doctors should supervise the nutrition of the prisoners more closely than before and submit proposals for improvements in conformance with the administrative measures of the camp commanders.

---

81 NG-2586.
82 NO-1523.

These should not only be put on paper, but should be regularly monitored by the camp medical doctors. [...] The Reichsführer SS has ordered that mortality absolutely must be reduced."

Himmler issued this order for the reduction of mortality at a time when, according to Hilberg and the other 'Holocaust' historians, six 'extermination camps' were running full blast, since gassing had supposedly begun two months before in Majdanek, the sixth 'death factory'. It could hardly be more clearly shown how the annihilation theory however framed has no connection with the facts backed by documentation.

In fact, the conditions in the camps improved markedly as a result of this directive and the mortality sank by almost 80% within eight months.[83]

On 26th October 1943, at a time when Hilberg tells us 4.3 million Jews had already been exterminated and the extermination of 800,000 more was yet to come (p. 1300; *DEJ*, na), Oswald Pohl sent a general notice to the commanders of 19 concentration camps, in which he stated:[84]

"In the framework of German armaments production, thanks to the improvement efforts that have been undertaken in the past 2 years, the concentration camps have become of decisive importance in the war. From nothing we have built armaments works that are second to none.

We now have to redouble our efforts to make sure that the production levels so far achieved are not only maintained, but further improved. That will be possible, as long as the works and factories remain intact, only by maintaining and even improving the labor capacity of the prisoners.

In earlier years, given the reeducational policy of the time, it did not matter much whether or not a prisoner could perform useful work. Now, however, the labor capacity of the prisoners is important, and all measures of the commanders, director of the liaison service and medical doctors should be extended to maintaining the health and efficiency of the prisoners. Not from phony sympathy, but because we need them with their arms and their legs, because they must contribute to a great victory for the German people, we must take the well-being of the prisoners to heart.

I want this to be the primary goal: no more than 10% of all prisoners should be unable to work due to sickness. All responsible persons should work together to achieve this goal. This will require:

1) proper and fitting nourishment,
2) proper and fitting clothing,
3) utilization of all natural health measures
4) avoidance of all effort not necessary for the performance of work,
5) performance bonuses."

---

83 PS-1469.
84 Archiwum Muzeum Stutthof I-1b-8, p. 53.

Just eight days later, on 3rd November 1943, Hilberg tells us, the Germans shot over 40,000 Jewish workers in Majdanek and two of its outlying camps (p. 559; *DEJ*, p. 532 states they shot "*as many as 17,000 workers in a single operation*")!

For 1944 also, we are in possession of a large number of documents which show the deployment of—mostly Jewish—prisoners in the armaments industry; on 11th May, for example, Adolf Hitler personally ordered the deployment of 200,000 Jews in the framework of the fighter plane construction program.[85] A few days later, Hilberg and his consorts again tell us, the first death trains with Hungarian Jews were on their way to Birkenau. Further comment would be superfluous.

Because of the large number of documents concerning the economic aspects of the deportations, it was not possible for Hilberg to simply skip the subject. He devotes 20 pages (pp. 550-570; *DEJ*, pp. 523-542) to the subject in connection with the deportation of Polish Jews and also provides several concrete examples of the utilization of Jewish labor. On p. 551 (*DEJ*, pp. 524f.), for example, he writes:

> "In Upper Silesia tens of thousands of Jews had been drawn from ghettos into camps by the Organisation Schmelt, an agency in charge of labor impressment in the Silesian region.[139] Thousands were employed in the construction of war plants. They were indispensable enough to cause Obergruppenführer Schmauser, the Higher SS and Police Leader of Upper Silesia, to write to Himmler in April 1942 that replacements for 6,500 Jews in major construction projects (Grossbauten) would hardly be available.[140] Several months later, when Krupp was planning to build a plant for the production of naval artillery at Markstädt, near Breslau, the firm discovered that the Organisation Todt (Speer's construction agency) was employing many Jews in projects nearby. With the 'complete approval' of Vizeadmiral Fanger, Krupp suggested that these Jews stay on to erect the naval factory.[141] In 1944 the Silesian Krupp plant was still employing thousands of these Jews.[142]"

On p. 564 (*DEJ*, p. 537) Hilberg provides a list of "*more important enterprises with Jewish labor forces*"; there are 17 firms on the list. (*DEJ* lists 16 firms)

The absurdity of the idea that the Germans urgently in need of laborers had wantonly annihilated an immense number of exactly these laborers is uncommonly embarrassing for the defenders of the extermination theory. They regularly resort to the argument that only Jews unfit for work were gassed and that those fit for work were left alive. This evasion utterly con-

---

85 NO-5689.

tradicts the assertion of these same historians that the Germans indiscriminately gassed all Jews irrespective of age or health in four to six extermination camps[86] and thereby destroyed many hundreds of thousands of potentially valuable laborers. If there had been an annihilation policy, there must have been some logic to it, but there is no recognizable logic to the policy that Hilberg and his consorts ascribe to the NS regime.

In order to alleviate these screaming contradictions somewhat, Hilberg invents internecine warfare within the NS leadership between the advocates of annihilation and its opponents. For example, on p. 552 (*DEJ*, p. 525) he asserts:

> "The year 1942 was a time when the civil administration, the Ostbahn, private firms under contract to the military commander or the Armament Inspectorate, as well as the SS itself, were all making use of Jewish labor in various business ventures. Foremost among the offices [sic] attempting to check the flow of irreplaceable Jewish workers into the killing centers were the military commander, General Gienanth, and the armament inspector, Generalleutnant Schindler."

No source is given, because the attempt to curb the disappearance of irreplaceable Jewish workers into the killing centers attributed to generals von Gienanth and Schindler is Hilberg's own *invention*. To prove that such an attempt had been made—naturally, without bothering about documentary support—Hilberg would first of all have had to produce evidence for the existence of the killing centers, and this he has still not done in 552 pages.

3. Hilberg's Invented Mass Shootings in Galicia

On p. 521 (*DEJ*, p. 496) the exalted high priest of the 'Holocaust' informs his readers as follows:

> "In Stanisławow [a town in Galicia], about 10,000 Jews had been gathered at a cemetery and shot on October 12, 1941. Another shooting took place in March 1942, followed by a ghetto fire lasting for three weeks. A transport was sent to Bełżec in April, and more shooting operations were launched in the summer, in the course of which Jewish council members and Order Service men were hanged from lampposts. Large transports moved out to Bełżec in September and October [...]"

Let us leave to one side the transports to Bełżec, the shooting in March 1942 and the Jews "*hanged from lampposts*", and content ourselves

---

86 In Treblinka, Bełżec, Sobibór and Chełmno supposedly only a handful of "*worker Jews*" (*Arbeitsjuden*) needed for the operation of the killing areas were excepted from immediate death.

with the first item of 'information' here, the shooting of not less than 10,000 Jews in the cemetery in Stanislavov on 12th October 1941. This number corresponds to the population of a small town. What evidence does Hilberg support himself with, what sources does he name as proof for the ten thousandfold murder in the cemetery? Simply and utterly none, not even a witness statement. In other words: The story is a pure chimera.

For the mass shooting of over 40,000 Jewish armaments workers that supposedly took place on 3rd November 1943 in Majdanek and its outlying camps Travniki and Poniatova, Hilberg at least gives us sources in the form of witness statements (p. 563; *DEJ*, p. 537). Italian researcher Carlo Mattogno was the first to investigate rigorously this supposed massacre—which has inexplicably entered the 'Holocaust' literature with the name "*harvest festival*" (*Erntefest*)—on a scientific basis and prove conclusively that it should be relegated to the realm of legend.[87]

4. As Sheep to the Slaughter…

If it is true that millions of Jews were killed in killing factories set up for that purpose, it would not have been possible to keep this a secret. Hilberg himself acknowledges this glaring fact. Concerning the 'extermination camps' Chełmno, Treblinka and Bełżec, for example, he writes:

> "*Poland* [...] *was the home of all six killing centers and Polish transports were moving in short hauls of not more than 200 miles in all directions. Many eyes were fixed on those transports and followed them to their destinations. The deputy chief of the Polish Home Army* [(a) *London-directed underground force), General Tadeusz Bór-Komorowski, reports that in the spring of 1942 he had complete information about the Kulmhof (Chełmno) killing center in the Warthegau.* [...] *In July 1942 the Home Army collected reports from railroad workers that several hundred thousand Jews had disappeared in Treblinka without a trace.*[...88]
>
> *Sometimes the information spilling out of the camps was quite specific. In the Lublin district the council chairman of the Zamość ghetto, Mieczysław Garfinkiel, was a recipient of such news. During the early spring of 1942 he heard that the Jews of Lublin were being transported in crowded*

---

87 Jürgen Graf and Carlo Mattogno, *KL Majdanek. Eine historische und technische Studie*, Castle Hill Publishers, Hastings 1997, pp. 211-232 (online: http://vho.org/D/Majdanek); English in preparation by Theses & Dissertations Press.

88 Hilberg is apparently not aware of the absurdity of this assertion, otherwise he would not quote it. Treblinka was opened in July 1942, as he notes on p. 956; the exact date was the 23rd July. (*Enzyklopädie des Holocaust, op. cit.* (note 36), v. III, p. 1430). This means that, according to Hilberg's 'railway workers', in this tiny camp within at most 8 days (23rd-31st July) *hundreds of thousands* of Jews 'disappeared without a trace'!

trains to Bełżec and that the empty cars were being returned after each trip for more victims. He was asked to obtain some additional facts and, after contacting the nearby Jewish communities of Tomaszów and Bełżec, was given to understand that 10,000 to 12,000 Jews were arriving daily in a strongly guarded compound located on a special railroad spur and surrounded by barbed wire. The Jews were being killed there in a 'puzzling manner'. Garfinkiel, an attorney, did not give credence to these reports. After a few more days, two or three Jewish strangers who had escaped from Bełżec told him about gassings in barracks. Still he did not believe what he heard. On April 11, 1942, however, there was a major roundup in Zamość itself. Counting the remaining population of his ghetto, Garfinkiel calculated a deficit of 3,150 persons. The next day, the thirteen-year-old son of one of the council functionaries (Wolsztayn) came back from the camp. They boy had seen the naked people and had heard an SS man make a speech to them. Hiding, still clothed, in a ditch, the young Wolsztayn had crawled out under the barbed wire with the secret of Bełżec.[40]" (pp. 517f.; *DEJ*, pp. 492f.)

Like a wildfire the news of the mass gassings must have spread over all Poland in these circumstances, and from there out into the bordering countries! How did the Jews now threatened with annihilation react to this Job's news? Raul Hilberg does not hide it from us:

"Throughout Poland the great bulk of the Jews presented themselves voluntarily at the collection points and boarded the trains for transport to killing centers. Like blood gushing out of an open wound, the exodus from the ghettos quickly drained the Polish Jewish community of its centuries-old life." (p. 520; *DEJ*, p. 495)

No, it is not complimentary, the testimony that Hilberg gives here about his 'race' or his fellow Jews! The descriptions of Jewish attempts at flight or resistance that follow this passage in no way blot out the monstrousness of the assertion that the great bulk of Jews voluntarily allowed themselves to be sent to the killing centers.

Again in August 1944, when almost the whole of Polish Jewry had been exterminated—as we are told by our 'Holocaust' pope—the Jews of the ghetto of Łódź boarded the trains to Auschwitz willingly and without resistance, because:

"In fact, Łódź had become the largest ghetto by default,[89] its 80,000 people struggling with a prison diet and a twelve-hour day for two more years. Then, in August 1944, announcements were posted in the ghetto under the heading 'Verlagerung des Ghettos (transshipment of the ghetto).'

---

89 The German-language edition states here that the growth was due to delays in deportation. But how can delays in deportation be explained when the 'extermination camp' Chełmno lay close by?

The Jews were ordered to present themselves for Verlagerung on penalty of death.[116]

This time the Jews knew where [German chief of the ghetto administration office] Biebow wanted to send them, and something like a sitdown strike ensued in workshops I and II. These Jews had held out for so long that now, with the end of the war in sight, they were not willing to go to their deaths voluntarily. The Germans decided to proceed with propaganda warfare. […] Biebow […] began to speak. […]

Biebow had always tried to do his best. He still wanted to do his best—namely, 'to save your lives by moving this ghetto'. Right now, Germany was fighting with her last ounce of strength. Thousands of German workers were going to the front. These workers would have to be replaced. Siemens and Schuckert urgently needed workers, Union needed workers, the Częstochowa munitions plants needed workers. […] The trip, said Biebow, was going to take ten to sixteen hours. Food had already been loaded on the trains. Everybody could take along 40 pounds of luggage. Everyone was to hold on to his pots, pans, and utensils, because in Germany such things were given only to bombed-out people. So, common sense. If not, and then force were used, Biebow could not help anymore.[117]

The Jewish workers of workshop areas I and II changed their minds. They surrendered. By the end of August the ghetto was empty except for a small cleanup Kommando.[118] The victims were shipped not to Germany, to work in plants, but to the killing center in Auschwitz, to be gassed to death.[119]" (p. 543; *DEJ*, pp. 517f.)

Were they dumb as straw or pathetically cowardly, the Jews of Łódź? They were the former if they believed the promises of their (alleged) executioners. They were the latter if they foresaw their destiny and nevertheless made no attempt to flee, or, if there were no chance for flight, at least to try to take as many of their executioners to death with them as they could. Like sheep they marched to the slaughter, we are told!

The Hungarian Jews did exactly the same thing, also in 1944. Thus Hilberg:

"in Hungary the Jews had survived until the middle of 1944. They were killed in Hitler's final year of power, in an Axis world that was already going down to defeat. […] The Hungarian Jews were almost the only ones who had full warning and full knowledge of what was to come while their community was still unharmed. Finally, the Hungarian mass deportations are remarkable also because they could not be concealed from the outside; they were carried out openly in full view of the whole world." (pp. 859f.; *DEJ*, p. 797)

On this subject Hilberg quotes Dr. Rudolf Kastner, former copresident of the Hungarian Zionist Association, as follows:

> *"In Budapest we had a unique opportunity to follow the fate of European Jewry. We had seen how they had been disappearing one after the other from the map of Europe. At the moment of the occupation of Hungary,* [meaning, March 1944] *the number of dead Jews amounted to over five million. We knew very well about the work of the Einsatzgruppen. We knew more than it was necessary about Auschwitz... We had, as early as 1942, a complete picture of what had been happening in the East with the Jews deported to Auschwitz and other extermination camps."* (p. 888; *DEJ*, p. 823)

On 19th March 1944 Adolf Eichmann and a few other *"deportations experts of the RSHA"* met in Budapest with the leaders of the Jewish community. On this meeting, Hilberg reports:

> *"During the meeting Eichmann performed one of the greatest shows of his career. In the words of the historian Levai, 'he virtually hypnotized the Jewish Council and through that body, the whole of Hungarian Jewry'*
>
> *Eichmann began his speech by giving the assembled Jews the bad news. First, he said, the Jewish labor battalions would have to be increased.*[90] *However, he assured his listeners that the Jewish workers would be treated well and that they might even be permitted to return home at night. Second, a Judenrat would have to be formed with jurisdiction over all Jews in Hungary. The Judenrat would have to act as a channel for German orders, as a central financing and taxation agency, and as a central depository of information concerning Hungarian Jews. Third, the Judenrat would have to publish a newspaper that would contain all the German orders.* [...]
>
> *So much, said Eichmann, for the German requests.* [...]
>
> *The Jews were relieved. Now they knew what they had to do. Falling all over each other, they began to draw up plans for their Judenrat.* [...]
>
> *At the same time, the council addressed a manifesto to the Jewish population to maintain discipline and obey orders:*
>
>> *On receiving orders from the Central Council it is the duty of every person to report at the place and time indicated."* (pp. 889f.; *DEJ*, pp. 824f.)

Let us recapitulate: The Hungarian Jews had *"full knowledge of what was to come"*; they had seen how the Jewish population groups had been *"disappearing one after the other from the map of Europe"*; since 1942, they had *"a complete picture of what had been happening in the East with the Jews deported to Auschwitz and other extermination camps"*—and what did the Jewish leaders do? They willingly undertook the role of *"channel for German orders"* and ordered the Jewish common people *"to report at the place and time indicated"* by the Central Council. Hilberg says the Jewish

---

90 After Hungary entered the war against the USSR on the side of the German Reich, Hungarian Jews were conscripted also. Certainly they did not serve under arms, but were organized into labor battalions.

community leaders had become "*a pawn in German hands*" (p. 890; *DEJ*, p. 825).

In other words, the Jewish leaders were cowardly evildoers who wittingly and willingly cooperated in the destruction of their people—assuming, of course, that Hilberg is right and that the purpose of the deportations really was the extermination of the deportees

5. People 'Gassed' in Auschwitz Turn up in Stutthof

Concentration camp Stutthof, lying 36 km (22.5 miles) east of Danzig—mentioned by Hilberg in his giant work only four times—is of overriding importance for the understanding of German Jewish policy in the next to last year of the war. Between June 29 and October 28, 1944, Stutthof received over 50,000 Jews, who were sent from the Baltic area (Kaunas and Riga) and also from Auschwitz.[91] Some of the deportation lists can be inspected at the archive of the Stutthof memorial.[92] Of the Jews who came from Auschwitz, 11,464 were from Łódź and 10,602 were from Hungary.[93] Also a considerable number of the Jews transported to Stutthof from Riga and Kaunas were Hungarian.[92] It is clear that they had been sent to the Baltic area first when they were deported from Hungary—possibly through the railway junction at Auschwitz—to be employed there on munitions projects, before the approach of the Red Army forced the Germans to retreat from the Baltic states and to evacuate the camps there.

At that time Stutthof performed the function of a major distribution center for labor forces; the—mostly female—Jewish prisoners were apportioned among the various outlying camps, transferred to camps further south or employed as agricultural labor.[94]

We have found that the transferees from Auschwitz to Stutthof constituted only a small proportion of the Hungarian Jews deported from Łódź and Hungary. The disposition of the others is mostly still unclear; as the archives in the East are opened to research, the subject may be progressively better understood. On the other hand, every Jew that left Auschwitz alive is a powerful argument against the theory that the latter served as an annihilation center for European Jewry. The transfers also square with the countless documents that deal with the deployment of Jews as labor. This

---

91 On this see Jürgen Graf and Carlo Mattogno, *op. cit.* (note 40).
92 Archiwum Muzeum Stutthof, I-II B- 11 (Transport lists).
93 Danuta Drywa, "*Ruch transportów między Stutthof i innymi obozami*", in: *Stutthof. Zeszyty Muzeum* (Stutthof. Museum Notebook), no. 9, Stutthof 1990, p. 17.
94 J. Graf and C. Mattogno, *op. cit.* (note 40), pp. 107-114.

also explains why Hilberg does not once mention the transfers to Stutthof, since they fail to support his presupposed exterminationist point of view.

The reason for the deportation of people from Łódź and Hungarian Jews was apparently that which the German chief of the ghetto administration office gave to the Jews of Łódź and which Adolf Eichmann gave in his meeting with the Hungarian-Jewish community leaders. The Jews were to be drafted as workers. Those that could not be employed at Auschwitz and its outlying camps were transferred to Stutthof—or to other camps or armaments works.

The Jews were aware of this. Had they known or even suspected that they faced cold-blooded murder, they would not have boarded the trains to Auschwitz. Of course, they were not the miserable weaklings that Hilberg so disparagingly portrays. Foreseeing certain death, they would definitely have taken any chance at escape or taken to arms in despair.

In other words, the community leaders of Łódź and the Hungarian Jews recognized the extermination and gassing stories which had been assiduously disseminated for years for what they were, namely war propaganda.

VII. The Killing Centers

1. The Initial Situation

From p. 927 (*DEJ*, p. 861) forward we confront the main theme of the 'Holocaust', namely the supposed mass killing of Jews in killing centers specially constructed for that purpose, which Hilberg characterizes as follows:

> *"The most striking fact about the killing center operations is that, unlike the earlier phases of the destruction process, they were unprecedented. Never before in history had people been killed on an assembly-line basis."* (p. 927; *DEJ*, p. 863)

In this chapter the central problem that has caused Hilberg so much trouble from the beginning of his second volume, namely, the complete lack of documentary evidence for the presence of such centers, assumes gigantic proportions. Every "*assembly-line*" in the world can be drawn, blueprinted, and photographed—except, it seems, Hilberg's.

No documentary paperwork has survived from the four 'pure extermination camps', Chełmno, Bełżec, Sobibór and Treblinka. The orthodox historians explain that this is because the Germans destroyed it in time. This certainly cannot be excluded—but then, why did the Germans carelessly leave behind stacks of records in Auschwitz and Majdanek? The court historians of the Allies never consider a second possibility, namely, that the Soviets and the Polish Communists captured German records in the four other 'extermination camps' as well as in Auschwitz and Majdanek, but got rid of them or let them disappear into secret archives because they too blatantly contradicted the desired propagandistic view of these camps.

For Bełżec, Hilberg mentions journals of Fritz Reuter, the deputy director of the Population and Welfare Subdivision of the Interior Division in the Office of the Gouverneur of Lublin. According to these journals, Hans Höfle, an assistant of Odilo Globocnik,[95] stated that a camp for Jews was to be built in Bełżec, on the Eastern border of the Generalgouvernement; the Jews would cross the border and would never return to the Generalgouvernement (pp. 940f.; *DEJ*, p. 878). Sobibór and Treblinka, like Bełżec, lay in the extreme east of the Generalgouvernement. Remembering

71

that German documents repeatedly speak of "*resettlement of the Jews to the east*" and that the occurrence of these resettlements is not denied even by the orthodox historians,[96] it is obvious that these camps might have been transit camps in which Jews were to be temporarily held pending transfer further east. Of course, Hilberg does not find such a hypothesis worthy of consideration.

Since no wartime German documents have survived from these three camps—or from Chełmno (Kulmhof), lying west of Łódź—and there are no material remains except for some barracks foundations in Chełmno, Hilberg is free to babble as much as he wants, supported by a few witness reports and also Adalbert Rückerl's frequently referenced book *Nationalsozialistische Vernichtungslager im Spiegel deutscher Strafprozesse,*[97] which itself is almost exclusively based on witness testimony given in Federal German trials. Hilberg is less free to do so in the case of Auschwitz and Majdanek. For one thing, the structures identified as killing gas chambers have partly survived, so one can examine them with respect to their suitability for the use ascribed to them. For another thing, in this case we are in possession of a large number of wartime records, and these do not contain any indication of a policy of annihilation or of killing gas chambers, but do contain much evidence for the economic significance of these camps.

In the subchapter "*Labor Utilization*" (pp. 982-1000; *DEJ*, pp. 917-935) Hilberg explores this topic in detail. On p. 985 (*DEJ*, p. 921) he summarizes "*SS Industry in the Killing Centers*" in a table, and on pp. 987-994 (*DEJ*, pp. 922-931) he discusses the activities of I.G. Farben in Auschwitz. Here are some excerpts:

> "*Significantly, the I.G.'s involvement in Auschwitz can be traced not to a desire to kill Jews or to work them to death but to a complicated manufacturing problem: the expansion of synthetic rubber (Buna) production* [in view of the lack of natural rubber required for tire manufacture and important for the war...]
>
> *The Ludwigshafen plant did not suffice to bring production to the required level, and the planners consequently considered two alternatives: expansion of the Hüls plant from 40,000 tons to 60,000 tons or construction*

---

95 SS-Brigadeführer Odilo Globocnik was a confidant of Himmler's and from June 1941 the person in charge of the construction of SS and police support points in the 'new Eastern region'. At the end of March 1942 he was assigned direction of "*Operation Reinhard*". As far as can be determined from the fragmentary documentation, the purpose of the latter was the seizure of property of deported Jews.

96 Cf. the comments in chapter V on the deportation of German and Czech Jews to White Russia and the Baltic region.

97 Published 1977 by dtv.

of another plant with a capacity of 25,000 tons. The new plant could be constructed in Norway or at Auschwitz.

From the beginning, the Economy Ministry pushed the Auschwitz site. [...] On February 6, 1941, [... I.G. Farben production chief Fritz] Ter Meer and the deputy chief of the main plant at Ludwigshafen, Dr. Otto Ambros, candidly talked over with [I.G. Farben officer Carl] Krauch the advantages and disadvantages of Auschwitz.

Ambros brought out the facts that Auschwitz had good water, coal and lime supplies. Communications were also adequate. Disadvantages were the lack of skilled labor in the area and the disinclination of German workers to live there.[26] [...]

On March 19 and April 24, 1941, the TEA[98] decided upon the details of Auschwitz production. There were to be two plants: a synthetic rubber plant (Buna IV) and an acetic acid plant. [...]

The investment in Auschwitz was initially over RM 500,000,000, ultimately over RM 700,000,000.[29] [...] About 170 contractors were put to work.[31] The plant was set up, roads were built, barracks were constructed for the inmates, barbed wire was strung for 'factory pacification' (Fabrikeinfriedung),[32] and, after the town of Auschwitz was flooded with I.G. personnel, two company villages were built.[33] To make sure that I.G. Auschwitz would have all the necessary building materials, Krauch patronizingly ordered that Buna enjoy first priority (Dringlichkeitsstufe I) until completion.[34] Spreading out, I.G. Auschwitz acquired its coal base, the Fürstengrube and the Janinagrube. Both mines were filled with Jewish inmates.[35]" (pp. 991ff.; *DEJ*, pp. 924f., 928f.)

Thus, the town of Auschwitz, bordering the concentration camp, "*was flooded with I.G. personnel*", "*170 contractors were put to work.*" Does this mean that the National Socialists did everything they could to see to it that news of the industrialized killing in Auschwitz would spread over all Europe in no time? But the world was silent. The Vatican was silent, the International Red Cross was silent and even the Allied governments, who routinely accused the Germans of all kinds of atrocities, never mentioned Auschwitz. Remarkable, is it not?

Although Hilberg generously concedes that the participation of I.G. Farben in Auschwitz "*can be traced not to a desire to kill Jews*", he claims "*the SS mentality had taken hold even of I.G. Farben directors*":

"*One day, two Buna inmates, Dr. Raymond van den Straaten and Dr. Fritz Löhner-Beda, were going about their work when a party of visiting I.G. Farben dignitaries passed by. One of the directors pointed to Dr. Löhner-Beda and said to his SS companion: 'This Jewish swine could work a lit-*

---

98 *"Technischer Ausschuß"* (Technical Committee).

*tle faster (*Diese Judensau könnte auch rascher arbeiten*).' Another director then chanced the remark: 'If they can't work, let them perish in the gas chamber (*Wenn die nicht mehr arbeiten könne, sollen sie in der Gaskammer verrecken*)'."* (p. 994; *DEJ*, p. 930)

This episode, in which an unnamed I.G. director threatens Jews who work too slowly with the gas chamber, is 'proven' by an affidavit made by former Auschwitz inmate van den Straaten on 18th July 1947 for one of the Nuremberg successor trials. This example is characteristic: The existence of *"the gas chamber"*[99] and the involvement of German industry in annihilation of the Jews is 'proven' by witness testimony given in an Allied trial. For the prosecutors and judges of defeated Germany, it was child's play to obtain such testimony. There was certainly no lack of former Jewish concentration camp prisoners who burned for revenge on their former oppressors, and there was no lack of typewriters and stationery on which to write down their 'affidavits'. This is the way in which most of Hilberg's evidence for the 'Holocaust' came into existence.

2. Hilberg's Imaginary Number of Victims of the 'extermination camps'

On p. 956 (*DEJ*, pp. 893, 894) Hilberg provides an overview of *"The 'Final Solution' in the Death Camps"*; he gives the following death counts:

in Chełmno:[100]	150,000 Jews
in Bełżec:	550,000 Jews
in Sobibór:	200,000 Jews
in Treblinka:	750,000 Jews
in Majdanek:[101]	50,000 Jews
in Auschwitz:	1,000,000 Jews
TOTAL:	2,700,000 Jews

Non-Jewish victims of these six camps Hilberg deems worthy only of a footnote (on p. 955; *DEJ*, p. 894) in which he asserts—without a source—that in Auschwitz more than 250,000 non-Jews, mostly Poles, perished; in Chełmno, Treblinka and Auschwitz he says tens of thousands of Gypsies were gassed, of course, without any evidence to support it.

The thoughtful reader would certainly like to know how Hilberg came by his figure of 2.7 million gassed Jews, but the reader's hopes remain

---

99 Note the singular!
100 Hilberg calls this camp by its German name Kulmhof.
101 Hilberg calls this camp by the name Lublin, which was also used in official NS communications.

unfulfilled: no sources of any kind are given—except for a reference to Danuta Czech's *Kalendarium*,[102] which, however, only discusses the *transports that arrived at Auschwitz* (p. 955; *DEJ*, p. 894). In other words, the numbers are humbug snatched out of thin air which Hilberg has copied down from various other unnamed authors and partially 'corrected' after his own personal taste.[103]

Robert Faurisson has rated Hilberg's work to be superior with respect to the amount of labor input, but with respect to its quality he calls it "*atrocious*" (*exécrable*).[104] In view of the shameless sleight-of-hand of the pope of the 'Holocaust', who can pull 2.7 million Jews murdered in six camps out of his sleeve without an iota of evidence, we have to concur with Faurisson's opinion. The fact that the work of other 'Holocaust' scribblers, such as Lucy Dawidowicz, who comes up with a total of more than 5 million Jews exterminated in the same six camps,[105] is of even worse quality is no excuse for Hilberg.

For Bełżec, Sobibór, Treblinka and Chełmno, without sources or material traces no rationally founded count of victims can be given. Even for Auschwitz, in 1985 Hilberg could not provide documentary evidence for his figure as he brought the "*definitive*" edition of his work to press, since at that time the death registers had not yet been made available from the Soviet archives. (Study of these death registers and of other documents which have become available in the meantime shows that the number of Jews and non-Jews who died in Auschwitz should be placed at somewhere between 160,000 and 170,000.[106]) For Majdanek, Hilberg could have found material with which to calculate an approximate number of victims (of Jews and non-Jews) had he taken the trouble to study the documents lying in the archive of the memorial at Majdanek.[107]

---

102 Danuta Czech, "*Kalendarium der Ereignisse im Konzentrationslager Auschwitz-Birkenau*", in: *Hefte von Auschwitz*, v. 2-4, 6-8 (1959-1964). At that time the staff of the Auschwitz Museum, which published D. Czech's study, were using a figure of four million Auschwitz victims, which Hilberg naturally does not mention. The 2nd edition of the *Kalendarium* was published by Rowohlt in 1989, four years after the definitive edition of Hilberg's work; English: *Auschwitz Chronicle: 1939-1945*, I.B. Tauris, London/New York 1990.

103 For Bełżec a victim count of 600,000 was given by all other standard works. Where Hilberg got his figure of 50,000 less he only knows.

104 Robert Faurisson, *Écrits révisionnistes*, *op. cit.* (note 3), p. 1892 (v. IV).

105 Lucy Dawidowicz, *The War against the Jews*, Penguin Books, New York 1975, p. 191. For Majdanek alone Dawidowicz claims 1.38 million Jewish victims, or twenty-seven times more than Hilberg!

106 Carlo Mattogno and Franco Deana, "*The Crematoria Ovens of Auschwitz and Birkenau*", in: Ernst Gauss (ed.), *op. cit.* (note 29), pp. 400. (online: http://codoh.com/found/fndcrema.html). As opposed to Hilberg, Mattogno and Deana *document* how they arrive at their number.

3. Killing Weapons and Removal of Corpses in the 'extermination camps', as Told by Hilberg

a. The 'Pure Extermination Camps'

Bełżec, Sobibór and Treblinka were apparently built by the Office of Buildings and Grounds of the SS-WVHA (which opened as Section C in March 1942).[108] Hilberg tells us, the sites *"were chosen with a view to seclusion and access to railroad lines"*. An inspection of the locations of the former camps reveals that in the case of Sobibór and Chełmno, not discussed here, one might talk of *"seclusion"*; Bełżec and Treblinka were situated only about a kilometer from towns of the same names, so that there would have been no possibility of keeping mass murder secret there. With respect to the gas chambers, Hilberg writes:

> *"Information about the number and size of gas chambers in each camp rests not on documentation but on recollection of witnesses. There is agreement that the new chambers were larger than the old (the capacity for simultaneous gassings in Bełżec during the summer of 1942 was estimated at 1,500). Counts of gas chambers are given in the following ranges:*
> *Bełżec   3, then 6*
> *Sobibór   3, then 4, 5, or 6*
> *Treblinka   3, then 6 or 10."* (footnote on p. 942; DEJ, p. 879)

In Chełmno, Hilberg says, Jews were killed in gas vans (p. 934; DEJ, p. 871). We have already said what has to be said about these mythical vehicles in connection with the events behind the eastern front, and there is no reason to add anything further.

On the gases used and removal of corpses, Hilberg states as follows:

> *"The gas first used at Bełżec was bottled, either the same preparation of carbon monoxide that had been shipped to the euthanasia stations or possibly hydrogen cyanide.[39]"* (p. 941; DEJ, p. 878)

In a footnote on the same page, he elaborates:

> *"Bottled gas (Flaschengas) is mentioned by Oberhauser (Obersturmführer at Bełżec). See text of his statement in Rückerl, NS-Vernichtungslager, pp. 136-137. The court judgement in the Oberhauser case identifies the gas as cyanide (Zyklon B), Ibid., p. 133."*

Hilberg continues:

---

107 Approximately 42,500 people died in Majdanek. Cf. Jürgen Graf and Carlo Mattogno, *op. cit.* (note 87), pp. 71-79. The percentage of Jews among the dead cannot be determined exactly, but it must have been over 50%. If one subtracts from Hilberg's claimed 50,000 Jewish victims of this camp the 17,000 or 18,000 invented shooting victims of 3rd November 1943, the resulting number is not much greater than the actual one.

108 *Wirtschaftsverwaltungshauptamt* (Main Office of Economic Administration).

> *"Later, all three camps (Sobibór and Treblinka from the start) were equipped with diesel motors. A German who briefly served at Sobibór recalls a 200-horsepower, eight-cylinder engine of a captured Soviet tank, which released a mixture of carbon monoxide and carbon dioxide into the gas chambers."* (p. 941; *DEJ*, p. 878)

Here is how he says the corpses were removed:

> *"In 1942 corpses were buried in mass graves in Kulmhof, the Generalgouvernement camps, and Birkenau. Before long this mode of dealing with the dead gave rise to second thoughts. [...] Ministerialrat Dr. Linden, sterilization expert in the Interior Ministry, on a visit to the Lublin district, is quoted by an SS man to have remarked that a future generation might not understand these matters.[98] The same consideration had prompted the Gestapo chief Müller to order Standartenführer Blobel, commander of Einsatzkommando 4a, to destroy the mass graves in the eastern occupied territories.[99] Blobel and his 'Kommando 1005' also moved into Kulmhof to investigate what could be done with the graves there. He constructed funeral pyres and primitive ovens and even tried explosives.[100][...]*
>
> *By 1942-1943 exhumations were in progress at all of the killing centers. In Kulmhof Jewish work parties opened the mass graves and dragged the corpses into newly dug pits and into a primitive oven.[105] In Bełżec the process was begun in the late fall of 1942 within a firing area of the camp capable of destroying 2,000 bodies per day. A second, somewhat smaller firing position was started a month later, and the two were used concurrently, day and night, until March 1943.[106] Excavators appeared in Sobibór and Treblinka, where the corpses (moved by narrow-gauge railway in Sobibór and dragged in Treblinka) were stacked and burned on firing grids built with old railway tracks.[107]"* (p. 1045; *DEJ*, pp. 976f.)

b. Majdanek

Hilberg gives no facts for the number and location of the gas chambers in the camp at Lublin. The gassings of persons were supposedly done with carbon monoxide.[109] Hilberg cautiously reports the assertion found in the Polish literature that in Majdanek the murders were also done with Zyklon B (footnote on p. 943; *DEJ*, p. 880). He says nothing about the methods of removal of corpses; in view of the small number of victims here compared to the other 'extermination camps', the question is of little importance.

---

109 Polish historical writings claim the carbon monoxide was fed to the gas chambers from steel bottles. Cf. J. Graf and C. Mattogno, *op. cit.* (note 87), chapter VI.

c. Auschwitz-Birkenau

A table on p. 946 (*DEJ*, p. 884) contains Hilberg's information on the gas chambers in this camp:

- One gas chamber in the crematory of the main camp (Auschwitz I);

- Bunker I, a former farmhouse in Birkenau, which contained five small gas chambers;[110]

- Bunker II, another former farmhouse in Birkenau;

- One underground gas chamber each in Crematories II and III in Birkenau, which began operations in March and June 1943, respectively;

- One above-ground gas chamber each in Crematories IV and V in Birkenau, which began operations in March and April 1943, respectively.

The killing weapon in Auschwitz was supposedly Zyklon B; Hilberg says the choice of this gas was made personally by camp commandant Rudolf Höß:

> "[Höß] *decided after visiting Treblinka that the carbon monoxide method was not very 'efficient'.*[55] *Accordingly, he introduced in his camp a different type of gas: quick-working hydrogen cyanide (prussic acid—commercial name, Zyklon).*" (p. 945; *DEJ*, p. 882)

In Birkenau, the real 'extermination camp', the corpses of the gassing victims as well as the corpses of those who died a natural death were incinerated in the four crematories which began operations starting March 1943 (pp. 947ff.; *DEJ*, p. 884). According to Hilberg, their theoretical daily capacity was over 4,000 (p. 1045; *DEJ*, p. 978).[111] In May and June 1944, Hilberg tells credulous readers, nearly 10,000 Jews were gassed every day, and in the second half of August even higher numbers were achieved. Since the capacity of the crematories was insufficient, the additional corpses were allegedly incinerated in pits (p. 1045f.; *DEJ*, p. 978).

---

110 Directly following the table in which Bunker I was said to have "*five small gas chambers*", Hilberg writes that "*the inner walls were removed*" from the two farm houses! If the inner walls were removed, it is logical that the house could have contained only one gas chamber and not five. Naturally, this would have simplified the gassing process and enlarged the usable area. Hilberg overlooks the fact that the removal of the inner walls would probably have caused the house to collapse, because in farm houses like this one the inner walls were usually load bearing walls.

111 According to the document Hilberg refers to—which we will discuss later—a further 340 corpses per day could be cremated in Crematory I of the main camp.

d. The Holocaust Pope with the Healthy Stomach

In any everyday murder trial an expert report is prepared on the weapon used to do the killing, be it a revolver or a knife, a hammer or an ax. In such a spectacular and inhuman crime as the claimed multiple million murders in 'extermination camps' one would expect to hear all the details about the weapon, meaning here not only the gas chambers but also the different gases. Let us recapitulate what Hilberg has said:

- For Treblinka and Sobibór the witnesses cannot even agree as to the number of gas chambers. A wise saying is: 'He who can swallow a toad without getting sick must have a strange stomach', and this applies to the Giant Hilberg.

- In Bełżec bottled gas was used at first, which was either carbon monoxide or hydrogen cyanide; Adalbert Rückerl's book on the Federal German NS trials says the latter was the case (*"The court judgement in the Oberhauser case identifies the gas as cyanide (Zyklon B)"*). Also the killers changed killing weapons and turned to a diesel motor.

- In Auschwitz, Rudolf Höß decided on Zyklon B, because in Treblinka he had noticed that the carbon monoxide method (meaning, use of a diesel motor which allegedly blew carbon monoxide into the gas chamber) was *"not very efficient"*. In this case, why would one have given up Zyklon B and turned to a diesel motor in Bełżec?

Hilberg swallows this toad also, without batting an eye. We continue: Zyklon B is not a 'bottled gas'; it is hydrogen cyanide adsorbed in a carrier substance (usually plaster of Paris)—occasionally used even today with the name *Cyanosil* for controlling harmful insects and rodents.[112] The product came in cans. When the cans were opened, the gas began to vaporize; the higher the temperature, the quicker the vaporization. Hilberg's remarks on Zyklon B (pp. 948f.; *DEJ*, pp. 884) show that he knows this. In that he quotes a Federal German court decision to the effect that Zyklon B was a *"bottled gas"*, he indirectly reveals that the Federal German court in question never took the trouble to determine what Zyklon B is by calling for an expert report on the murder weapon, in the course of a trial that concerned 550,000 to 600,000 murder victims—which speaks volumes as to the evidentiary value of such trials.

---

112 On this cf. Wolfgang Lambrecht, *"Zyklon B – eine Ergänzung"*, *VffG*, 1(1) (1997), pp. 2-5 (online: http://vho.org/VffG/1997/1/Lambrecht1.html)

We move on to Rudolf Höß, the first commandant of Auschwitz. Höß found the method of mass murder with diesel exhaust gases used in Treblinka not efficient enough and decided to use Zyklon in Auschwitz. As source for this, Hilberg gives Höß' affidavit made on 5th April 1946.[113]

Let us examine the chronology of events. On p. 946 (*DEJ*, p. 884) Hilberg tells us the mass gassings began in Auschwitz I in "*early 1942*" and in Bunker 2 in Birkenau in "*spring 1942*". Ten pages later, on p. 956 (*DEJ*, p. 893), he gives July 1942 as the date on which Treblinka began operations. Thus, Höß began gassing with Zyklon in *early 1942* in Auschwitz I and in *spring 1942* in Birkenau after he had convinced himself in July 1942, at the earliest, that the method used in Treblinka was not effective enough. Logical, is it not?

As to the removal of corpses in Bełżec between late fall 1942 and March 1943, 550,000 corpses were allegedly incinerated *under open sky*. This method must have been unusually successful, because certainly no one has been able to find any human remains to speak of on the site of the former camp. Why was this efficient method of removal of corpses not adopted in Auschwitz, why was the firm Topf and Sons brought in to build crematories with good money? How useless the construction of the latter was, was shown in May, June and August 1944, when in Birkenau 10,000 or so corpses *per day*, in August even more, needed to be incinerated: The open pits dug there "*broke the bottleneck*" (p. 1046; *DEJ*, p. 978). Since, as Hilberg tells us, the theoretical maximum capacity of the Birkenau crematories was rated at a little more than 4,000 corpses per day, the remaining up to 6,000 corpses per day must have been incinerated in the pits. Why then the useless crematories—a couple more pits would have done as well?

Hilberg's stomach is strong enough. He swallows one toad after another and never has a stomach ache.

4. Hilberg's Methodology: The Revaluation of all Values

In the discipline of jurisprudence there is a generally recognized hierarchy of evidence. At the top of the hierarchy is physical evidence, the investigation of the material traces of a crime (corpse, murder weapon, bloodstains, fingerprints and so on); the next highest rank is documentary evidence and the lowest is testamentary evidence, of which a particular form of testamentary evidence, the testimony of interested parties—those

---

113 PS-3868.

directly affected by the event in question—is considered particularly unreliable.[114]

With Hilberg, the ordering is reversed: Testamentary evidence and especially the testimony of interested parties is highest in the hierarchy, followed by documentary evidence. Physical evidence he does not bother with.

If a document contradicts a witness' statement, Hilberg regularly decides for the latter, as long as it will help his annihilation theory. Every historical researcher with a reputation for worthwhile work knows that in a conflict between documents and witnesses the former must be chosen. The—anti-Revisionist—French historian Jacques Baynac has remarked pointedly:[115]

> "For the scientific historian a witness statement does not represent real history. It is an object of history. A witness statement counts for little, many witnesses' statements count for no more, if there is no solid document to support them. One could say without much exaggeration, the principle of scientific historiography is, No paper(s), no proven facts."

Since Baynac's view is a generally held view in academic and judicial circles, these few sentences alone are enough to shatter to pieces Hilberg's chapter on the *"Killing Center Operations"*!

A pregnant example of the reversal of the scientifically recognized hierarchy of forms of evidence can be seen in those passages in which Hilberg discusses the disinfestation agent Zyklon B. This agent was employed in many camps—even those not claimed to be extermination camps—to eradicate lice, which transmitted typhus. The sometimes terrifying high death counts in the concentration camps[116] were due primarily to this rampaging disease.

On p. 949 (*DEJ*, p. 886) Hilberg writes:

> "The SS did not manufacture Zyklon, so the gas had to be procured from private firms. The enterprises that furnished it were part of the chemical industry. They specialized in 'combating of vermin' (Schädlingsbekämpfung) by means of poison gases. Zyklon was one of eight products manufactured by these firms,[71] which undertook large-scale fumigations of buildings, barracks, and ships; disinfected [sic] clothes in specially constructed gas chambers (Entlausungsanlagen); and deloused human beings,

---

114 On the hierarchy of evidence see Manfred Köhler, "*The Value of Testimony and Confessions Concerning the Holocaust*", in: Ernst Gauss (ed.), *op. cit.* (note 29), pp. 85-91 (online: http://codoh.com/found/fndvalue.html).

115 *Le Nouveau Quotidien*, Lausanne, 3rd September 1997.

116 In Auschwitz in late summer 1942 the epidemic sometimes claimed more than 300 lives per day. Cf. the statistics in Jean-Claude Pressac, *Les crématoires d'Auschwitz*, CNRS, Paris 1993, p. 145.
In Majdanek in August 1943 the death rate for men was 7.67% and for women 4.41%. (PS-1469).

protected by gas masks.[72] In short, this industry used very powerful gases to exterminate rodents and insects in enclosed spaces."

As his source for this information Hilberg names a lecture given 27th February 1942 by two gas experts, Dr. Gerhard Peters and Heinrich Sossen-heimer.[117] He also mentions (in footnote 70 on p. 949; *DEJ*, p. 886) a user manual with the title *Richtlinien für die Anwendung von Blausäure (Zyklon) zur Ungeziefervertilgung (Entwesung)* (Directive for Utilization of Zyklon for Extermination of Vermin)—also dating from 1942.[118]

The wartime German documents he quoted make it perfectly clear that Zyklon B was for purposes of disinfestation and for nothing else. This does not hinder Hilberg from writing:

> *"The amounts [of Zyklon B] required by Auschwitz were not large, but they were noticeable. Almost the whole Auschwitz supply was needed for the gassing of people; very little was used for fumigation.[85]"* (pp. 952f.; *DEJ*, pp. 889f.)

Hilberg's informant in this matter is the Rumanian Jew Charles Sigismund Bendel, a former Auschwitz prisoner to whom we will return.

Interestingly, in 1989 Jean-Claude Pressac turned Hilberg's statement upside down when he wrote that 97 to 98% of the Zyklon was used for pest control, and only 2 to 3% was used to kill Jews.[119]

That Hilberg gives more weight to the witnesses than to the documents is in and of itself inexcusable, and the delinquency is magnified by the fact that in almost all cases it is a case of testimony of interested parties, who tend to be particularly unreliable: Most of the witnesses he quotes were former Jewish concentration camp inmates, from whom objectivity on the subject of the Germans and especially the SS could not be expected, and who were only too happy to give testimony in trials that would put those who had deprived them of their freedom on the gallows or at least in prison.

But there is worse: Hilberg picks his witness statements so that they will support his predetermined dogma. By 1961, when he published his work for the first time, the currently accepted 'Holocaust' theory had already crystallized there: The mass murders were committed with gas in six extermination camps. One year before, Martin Broszat, then a researcher at the Institute for Contemporary History in Munich and later its director,

---

117 NO-9098.
118 NO-9912. The complete text of the document can be found in Herbert Verbeke (ed.) *Auschwitz: Nackte Fakten. Eine Erwiderung an Jean-Claude Pressac*, V.H.O., Berchem 1995, pp. 94-99 (online: http://vho.org/D/anf/Faurisson.html; Engl.: vho.org/GB/Books/anf/Faurisson1.html#h7).
119 Jean-Claude Pressac, *Auschwitz: Technique and Operation of the Gas Chambers*, Beate Klarsfeld Foundation, New York 1989, p. 188.

had declared that there had been no gassing of humans in Dachau, Bergen-Belsen, Buchenwald and other camps in the west.[120]

Hilberg holds fast to his prescribed view of the 'Holocaust', and he does not think it worthwhile to mention the numerous unreliable witness statements describing gassings in just these camps in the west.[121] He also refuses to discuss the alleged gas chambers at Mauthausen and Stutthof, although the former are tenaciously defended in Austria and the latter in Poland to the present day. In other words, Hilberg thinks that all testimonies on these gas chambers are false, meaning that the witnesses are lying or are subject to hallucinations. *Why then are the witness statements on gassings in the six 'extermination camps' a priori credible?* Hilberg will not touch crucial questions like this one even fleetingly.

If one were to put the witness testimony to mass murder of Jews coming from during and after the war under a magnifying glass, one would discover that there have been descriptions of all kinds of methods of killing which later have been forgotten. In a book published in 1945 a Dr. Stefan Szende described how millions of Jews were killed by electricity in Bełżec: The victims were made to stand on a metal plate, this was lowered into an underground water cistern, then high-voltage current was fed through the water. At that point, "*the metal plate became a crematory casket, glowing hot, until all the corpses were burnt to ashes*".[122] Simon Wiesenthal also claimed that Jews had been killed by electricity in Bełżec, but he described the killing process quite differently from Szende:[123]

> "*Crowded together, driven on by the SS, Latvians and Ukrainians, the people ran through the open gate into the 'bath'. It could hold 500 people at a time. The floor of the 'bathing room' was made of metal and there were shower heads in the ceiling. When the room was full, the SS switched the electricity, 5,000 volts, through the metal plate. At the same time the shower heads spurted water. A short scream, and the execution was over.*"

According to Wiesenthal, the corpses of those murdered in this way in Bełżec were made into soap:[124]

> "*At the end of 1942 there came for the first time the horrifying cry: 'Transport for soap!' It was in the Generalgouvernement, and the factory was in Galicia, in Bełżec. From April 1942 to May 1943 900,000 Jews were used as raw material in this factory.*"

---

120 *Die Zeit*, 19th August 1960.
121 One collection of such witness statements is contained in Jürgen Graf, *Der Holocaust-Schwindel*, Guideon Burg Verlag, Basel 1993, chapter 9.
122 Stefan Szende, *Der letzte Jude aus Polen*, Europa Verlag, Zürich/New York 1945, pp. 290ff.
123 *Der neue Weg*, Vienna, no. 19/20, 1946.
124 *Der neue Weg*, Vienna, no. 17/18, 1946.

As has already been mentioned, Hilberg calls the soap from Jewish fat a myth (pp. 1032f; *DEJ*, p. 967), and apparently, Hilberg must hold Wiesenthal to be a mythmaker. Yet another version of mass murder in Bełżec was given during the war by the Pole Jan Karski, who claimed that Jews were stuffed into goods trains and dusted with quicklime which slowly ate the flesh from their bones:[125]

> *"From one end to the other, the train, with its quivering cargo of flesh, seemed to throb, vibrate, rock, and jump as if bewitched."*

Another witness, the Polish Jew Rudolf Reder, said a gasoline motor was used to kill in Bełżec.[126] Although such a thing would be a much better killing device than a diesel motor,[127] Hilberg decided to support the latter, based on the testimony of Kurt Gerstein given in *Nationalsozialistische Massentötungen durch Giftgas* (p. 941; *DEJ*, na).

This—incomplete—overview of the witness statements provided the following as methods of killing used at Bełżec:

- killing by means of electricity in an underground water cistern, followed by incineration of the corpses (Szende);
- killing by means of electricity on a metal plate, followed by processing of the corpses into soap (Wiesenthal);
- killing in trains by means of quicklime (Karski);
- killing by means of carbon monoxide in bottles (unnamed witness cited by Hilberg on p. 941; *DEJ*, na);
- killing by means of Zyklon B in bottles (decision of a Federal German court, cited by Adalbert Rückerl);
- killing by exhaust gas from a gasoline motor (Reder);
- killing by exhaust gas from a diesel motor (Gerstein).

Hilberg settled on the fourth and the seventh variants—*why?*

Here is an overview of the killing methods testified to by various witnesses for Sobibór, Treblinka and Auschwitz, where we show the variant preferred by Hilberg in bold-face:

SOBIBÓR:

- a spirally, black substance dripping through holes in the ceiling of a death chamber camouflaged as a shower (Alexander Pechersky[128]);

---

125 Jan Karski, *Story of a Secret State*, The Riverside Press, Cambridge 1944, p. 350.
126 Rudolf Reder, *Bełżec*, Cracow 1946, p. 44.
127 See chapter VII.5.a.
128 A. Pechersky, "*La rivolta di Sobibór*", in: Yuri Suhl, *Ed essi si ribellarono. Storia della resistenza ebrea contro il nazismo*, Milan 1969, p. 31.

- Exhaust gas from a diesel motor (Léon Poliakov;[129] *Enzyklopädie des Holocaust*[130]);
- **Exhaust gas from a gasoline motor** (confession of SS-Unterscharführer Erich Fuchs in a post-war trial, quoted by Hilberg on p. 941; *DEJ*, na).

TREBLINKA:
- suffocation by pumping the air out of a death chamber (Wassili Grossman[131]);
- scalding with hot steam (Report of a Polish commission present at the Nuremberg Tribunal in December 1945[132]);
- killing by shooting in the neck on a conveyor belt (*Blackbook* of the Jewish World Congress[133]);
- **Exhaust gas from a diesel motor** (Hilberg, citing the witness statements in the collection *Nationalsozialistische Massentötungen durch Giftgas*, p. 941; *DEJ*, na).

AUSCHWITZ:
- electrified baths, a pneumatic hammer, war gas (report of the Polish resistance movement during the war[134]);
- an electrified conveyor belt (Jewish Soviet reporter Boris Polevoi in *Pravda* on 2nd February 1945);
- incineration while still alive in an oven, into which the condemned were dumped from a car (Eugène Aroneanu[135]);
- incineration while still alive in pits (Elie Wiesel[136]);
- **killing with Zyklon B** (dominant variant since spring 1945).

A look at the points in time when these various methods of killing were asserted is very eye-opening. For example, the Polish commission at the Nuremberg victor's tribunal responsible for providing 'evidence' for the mass murder in Treblinka settled on hot steam as the killing weapon *in*

---

129 L. Poliakov, *Harvest of Hate*, Holocaust Library, New York 1979, p. 196.
130 *Op. cit.* (note 36), v. III, p. 1496.
131 *Die Hölle von Treblinka*, Foreign Language Publication House, Moscow 1947, partially quoted by Udo Walendy in *"Der Fall Treblinka"*, *Historische Tatsachen*, no. 44, Verlag für Volkstum und Zeitgeschichtsforschung, Vlotho 1990. Grossman also reports steamings and gassings.
132 PS-3311.
133 *The Black Book—The Nazi Crime against the Jewish People*, Reprint Nexus Press, New York 1981, p. 398. The Black Book reports steamings, gassings and suffocations.
134 This report was quoted in its entirety by Enrique Aynat in *Estudios sobre el "Holocausto"*, Gráficas Hurtado, Valencia 1994.
135 Eugène Aroneanu, *Camps de Concentration*, Office Français d'Edition, Paris 1945, p. 182.
136 Elie Wiesel, *Night*, New York, Hill and Wang, 1960, p. 42.

December 1945, more than two years after the closing of the camp. This means it took the Poles more than two years to find out how several hundred thousand people were murdered in a camp only about one kilometer distant from the town of the same name—despite the fact that the town swarmed with Treblinka survivors.[137] Any comment would be superfluous.

Hilberg swallows all these toads contentedly. He ignores flat out the thousands of contradictions in the witness statements that are his only evidentiary foundation for the 'Holocaust', because he has determined the correct variant for every camp by decree: *Hilberg dixit...*[138]

a. Hilberg's Star Witnesses

We will now look a little closer at a few of the sources for gassing of Jews named in the chapter *"Killing Center Operations"* (pp. 927-1057; *DEJ*, pp. 861-990). It will be seen that Hilberg is blind to the grossest absurdities in his citations.

For every source we tell how often Hilberg cites it in his 130-pages section and we identify the footnotes that refer to the sources. Since one footnote might mention two or more sources, some footnotes appear several times.

Here then are Hilberg's sources:

ADALBERT RÜCKERL:

Rückerl is a former director of the Ludwigsburg Central Office for Prosecution of NS Crimes and author of the book *Nationalsozialistische Vernichtungslager im Spiegel deutscher Strafprozesse*. Hilberg names this work as a source forty-one times.[139] It illustrates better than anything else how all evidence for the 'Holocaust' rests on witness testimony—mostly given in trials—and how Federal German justice has not bothered with physical evidence. For his part, Rückerl cites the first edition of Hilberg's work copiously. One hand washes the other.

---

137 Numerous former Treblinka prisoners are quoted in Alexander Donat's *The Death Camp Treblinka* (Holocaust Library, New York 1979).

138 Latin for 'Hilberg spoke'. This appeal to his authority contradicts all academic traditions where only evidence is accepted as proof, but not reference to alleged authority or reputation.

139 Hilberg's footnotes 35, 40f., 43f., 113-116, 118, 120, 123ff., 405f., 412, 416, 422ff., 427, 429-434, 437, 439f., 458, 461, 464, 474, 482ff., 498, 502f.; Hilberg's *DEJ* footnotes 879(42, 43), 895(7), 896(10, 11, 12), 897(13, 14, 15, 17), 898(20, 21), 916(94), 968(30, 31), 969(37, 38), 970(41, 45, 46, 47), 971(50, 52, 53, 54, 55, 56, 57, 60), 972(62, 63, 65), 974(81, 84), 975(87), 976(97), 977(105, 106, 107), 979(4, 8).

FILIP FRIEDMAN:

Member of a Polish-Communist commission which published a 'documentation' of Auschwitz; it was first published in Yiddish and then in English with the title, *This Was Oswiecim*. Hilberg used the book as a source six times.[140] Here is a tasty morsel from this Stalinistic propaganda piece:[141]

> "This means that if we include 1941, the Oswiecim [Polish name for Auschwitz] death factory swallowed up over 5,000,000 people, and according to some accounts 7,000,000."

Hilberg, who had determined the number of Auschwitz victims to be 1.25 million (one million Jews and 250,000 non-Jews), does not balk at using F. Friedman's book as a serious source, which speaks of 5 to 7 million.

RUDOLF HÖSS:

Höß was the first commandant of Auschwitz and is the indispensable prime witness of the mass annihilation in that camp. Hilberg refers to him twenty-six times.[142]

In his confession given during an intensive three-day interrogation by a British torture team led by the Jewish Sergeant Bernard Clarke,[143] the first Auschwitz commandant stated that already by November 1943 in Auschwitz 2.5 million persons had been gassed and a further 500,000 had died of sickness, starvation and other factors.[144] Naturally Hilberg—who picks and chooses his statistics to suit his fancy—does not mention these statements, since these crassly exaggerated numbers, large even by Hilberg's standards, show that the Höß confession was not voluntarily given and is therefore worthless.

In his 'confession', Höß stated further that he had visited the Treblinka camp—remember it was opened in July 1942—in June 1941 and talked about a camp called "*Wolzek*", which has never been heard of since.

---

140 Hilberg's footnotes 44, 144, 166, 384, 459, 491; Hilberg's *DEJ* footnotes 879(43), 905(41), 967(27), 978(114).

141 Filip Friedman, *This Was Oswiecim*, The United Jewish Relief Appeal, London 1946, p. 14.

142 Hilberg's footnotes 49, 50, 55, 58, 60, 86, 91, 101, 130, 132, 136, 213, 238, 255ff., 381, 436, 452, 477, 481, 486, 490, 493, 540, 544; Hilberg's *DEJ* footnotes 49, 50 (p. 881), 55 (p. 882), 57, 59 (p. 883), 84 (p. 889), 97, 99 (p. 892), 29 (p. 901), 90 (p. 915), 4 (p. 918), 16 (p. 922), 40 (p. 929), 57, 58, 59 (p. 933), 61 (p. 934), 6 (p. 963), 14 (p. 964), 75 (p. 973), 91 (p. 975), 100, 104 (p. 977), 113, 116 (p. 978), 46, 50 (p. 987).

143 On the torture of Rudolf Höß see Rupert Butler, *Legions of Death*, Arrow Books, London 1983, pp. 235ff.; British special agent Vera Aitkins has also tortured Höß in order to receive 'confessions', cf. the Belgian newspaper *De Morgen*, Flanders, July 1, 2000.

144 PS-3868.

When he was turned over to Poland, he was put in the Cracow prison, where he wrote his 'memoirs', in which he penned down what he was told by his jailers.[145] In my book *Auschwitz. Tätergeständnisse und Augenzeugen des Holocaust*,[146] I have pointed out no less than 33 impossible things in these 'memoirs', and these are certainly not all of them.

RUDOLF VRBA:

Although the Slovakian Jew Vrba (originally Walter Rosenberg) is considered one of the main witnesses to the claimed extermination of the Jews in Auschwitz, Hilberg names him as a source only twice in the chapter on the *"Killing Center Operations"*.[147] After he and his fellow countryman and Jew Alfred Wetzler succeeded in escaping from Auschwitz in April 1944, they wrote a report which was published with other such reports in November of that year as the *"War Refugee Board Report"*, in which for the first time the stories of mass gassing with Zyklon B are spoken of. It can be ascertained from the report that Vrba and Wetzler never saw the crematories which contained the gas chambers because the map they drew does not in the least conform to the actual configuration of the crematories. They assert, for example, that the *Leichenkeller* (the alleged 'gas chamber') of Krema II was at the same level as the oven room, but in fact it was underneath the latter; also the number of ovens is wrong.[148]

Vrba 'corrects' these errors in his 1964 'factual report' *I Cannot Forgive*,[149] which Hilberg cites; he fantasizes about a Himmler visit in Auschwitz in January 1943 during which the Birkenau crematory was inaugurated with the gassing of 3,000 Jews[150] (in the WRB Report he had given the number 8,000). Later, we will quote a passage from the description of this gassing. In fact, the first crematory in Birkenau was opened in March 1943 (Hilberg, p. 946; *DEJ*, p. 884), and we know that Himmler visited Auschwitz for the last time in July 1942.[151] During the first Zündel trial in Toronto (1985), Vrba made a terrible fool of himself as witness for the prosecution. When Zündel's attorney Douglas Christie pressed him hard, he conceded he had allowed himself *"poetic licence"*.[152]

---

145 Rudolf Höß, *Kommandant in Auschwitz*, edited by M. Broszat, dtv, 1983.
146 Published by Neue Visionen, Würenlos 1994, pp. 74-81 (online: http://vho.org/D/atuadh).
147 Hilberg's footnotes 193 and 456; Hilberg's *DEJ* footnotes 90 (p. 915), 79 (p. 974).
148 On the WRB Report (also called the 'Auschwitz Protocols') see Enrique Aynat, *Los protocolos de Auschwitz - ¿Una fuente histórica?*, Garcia Hispán, Alicante 1990.
149 Published by Bantam, Toronto 1964.
150 *Ibid.*, pp. 10ff.
151 Jean-Claude Pressac, *op. cit.* (note 116), 1993, pp. 44.
152 Transcript of the 1st Zündel trial in Toronto, 1985, pp. 320ff., partially quoted in J. Graf, *Auschwitz. Tätergeständnisse...*, *op. cit.* (note 146), pp. 251-255.

Olga Lengyel:

Hilberg names the Hungarian Jewess O. Lengyel as a source seven times.[153] In her book *Five Chimneys* she writes that the crematories of Birkenau could incinerate 17,280 corpses in a 24-hours period. The theoretical maximum capacity was 1,000 per day.[154] She says the four *"ovens"* (by which she presumably means the crematories) had 120 *"openings"*—in fact, the crematories had together 46 muffles. With the help of the incineration pits, she says, 24,000 corpses per day were disposed of. In Birkenau for the period between the beginning of May and the 26th July 1944 alone, she says 1,314,000 persons were exterminated.[155] As we have seen, Hilberg comes to a figure of 1.25 million victims for the whole period of existence of Auschwitz-Birkenau (counting both persons exterminated and natural deaths). Lengyel also resorts to the nonsense about the industrial utilization of human fat:[156]

> *"The Nordic Supermen knew how to profit from everything. Immense casks were used to gather the human grease which had melted down at high temperatures. It was not surprising that the camp soap had such a peculiar odor. Nor was it astonishing that the internees became suspicious at the sight of certain pieces of fat sausage!"*

Elie Wiesel:

This witness, possibly the most famous of all 'Holocaust' star witnesses, Hilberg gives as a source only twice.[157] The Romanian Jew Wiesel was interned from April 1944 to January 1945, first in Birkenau and then in the main camp Auschwitz. In his 'factual report' *La Nuit* he does not mention the gas chambers even once[158]—at a time when hundreds of thousands of Jews were supposedly being gassed in Birkenau, 1.314 million according to his fellow Jew Olga Lengyel! Wiesel's story is that the Jews were pushed—or marched willingly—into flaming pits:[159]

---

153 Hilberg's footnotes 184, 187f., 428, 448, 451, 453; Hilberg's *DEJ* footnotes 81, 84, 85 (p. 913), 51 (p. 971), 71 (p. 972), 76 (p. 973).

154 That entails uninterrupted operation under ideal conditions, perhaps with the attendance of a qualified engineer. In fact, there were frequent stoppages due to needed repairs and the plant was amateurishly operated by unqualified persons, leading to a considerably lower capacity. On this, see Carlo Mattogno and Franco Deana, *op. cit.* (note 106), and also chapter VII.5.e in this book.

155 Olga Lengyel, *Five Chimneys*, Chicago/New York 1947, pp. 68ff.

156 *Ibid.*, pp. 72ff.

157 Hilberg's footnotes 447, 516; Hilberg's *DEJ* footnotes 70 (p. 972), 22 (p. 983).

158 In the German version published by Ullstein in 1990 with the title *Die Nacht zu begraben, Elischa* gas chambers, which are not mentioned in the original edition, suddenly appear: whenever *crématoire* had appeared in the French text, translator Meyer-Clason makes it a *"Gaskammer"*!

159 Elie Wiesel, *op. cit.* (note 136), p. 42.

> *"Our line had now only fifteen paces to cover. I bit my lips so that my father would not hear my teeth chattering. Ten steps still. Eight. Seven. We marched slowly on, as though following a hearse at our own funeral. Four steps more. Three steps. There it was now, right in front of us, the pit and its flames."*

He who wants to know how Wiesel miraculously escaped death in the fiery pit—time after time!—will find this book to his liking.

DR. MIKLOS NYISZLI:

The Jewish doctor Nyiszli—whom Hilberg names as a source four times[160]—was interned in Auschwitz, where he *claims* he worked as a medical doctor alongside Dr. Josef Mengele. In 1946 he wrote a 'factual report' in Hungarian which was translated into many languages and republished in 1992 with the title *Im Jenseits der Menschlichkeit.* Nyiszli says that in Birkenau 20,000 persons *per day* were gassed and incinerated in the crematories—the actual theoretical maximum capacity being smaller by more than twenty times. He knows nothing of the farm houses converted to gas chambers in Birkenau, called the "*bunkers*", but he reports that *beside* one farm house serving as a disrobing area, 5,000 to 6,000 persons were allegedly driven into blazing pits and burned alive every day.[161]

CHARLES SIGISMUND BENDEL:

Hilberg acknowledges this Romanian-Jewish medical doctor—named as source twice[162]—as the source of his information that most of the Zyklon B delivered to Auschwitz was used for extermination of the Jews. Bendel was a witness for the prosecution in the 1946 trial the British instituted against Dr. Bruno Tesch, the founder and director of Degesch (*Deutsche Gesellschaft für Schädlingsbekämpfung*), and his assistent Karl Weinbacher, where he contributed significantly to sending these two innocent men to the gallows (a third accused, Dr. Joachim Drosihn, was acquitted). Here is a passage from Bendel's examination by British major G.I.D. Draper:[163]

> *"Question: Do you know the total number of people exterminated in Auschwitz during the entire time the camp existed?*

---

160 Hilberg's footnotes 240, 466f., 470; Hilberg's *DEJ* footnotes 42 (p. 930), 89, 90 (p. 975).
161 Miklos Nyiszli, *Im Jenseits der Menschlichkeit*, Dietz Verlag, Berlin 1992, pp. 59ff.; At the 13th International Revisionist Conference in May 2000 (Irvine, CA), Charles Provan presented new interesting research about Nyiszli's background and fate, which will hopefully be published soon in both *The Journal of Historical Review* and *VffG*.
162 Hilberg's footnotes 87 and 467; Hilberg's *DEJ* footnotes 85 (p. 890), 90 (p. 975).
163 NI-11953.

Answer: Over four million.

Question: During your time there, what was the highest number of gassed persons in Birkenau on any single day?

Answer: In June [1944] *25,000 people were gassed day by day. Question: With gas?*

Answer: With hydrogen cyanide. [...] *There were two rooms in each crematory. In crematories 1 and 2* [the usual designation is now II and III] *they drove 1,000 persons into one room, so that both gas chambers together held 2,000 persons.*

Question: How big were the rooms?

Answer: Every gas chamber was 10 m long and 4 m wide. The people were pressed so closely together that not one more person could be squeezed in. The SS thought it was uproariously funny to throw children in over the heads of those already jammed in these rooms. [...] *The corpses were thrown into mass graves, but their hair was cut off and their teeth were pulled out, I saw it.*

Question: Was only the gold saved, or all the teeth?

Answer: The National Socialist government said, it put no store in gold; despite that, they were able to take 17 tons of gold from 4 million corpses."

Subsequently Bendel was cross-examined by Dr. Zippel, the attorney for the accused:

"Question: You have said, the gas chambers were 10 x 4 x 1.6 m large; is that correct?

Answer: Yes.

Question: That is 64 m^3, is it not?

Answer: I am not quite sure, that is not my strong point.

Question: How can it be possible to fit 1,000 people in a 64 m^3 room?

Answer: That's what you have to ask yourself. It can only be done with German methods.

Question: Do you seriously maintain that you can fit ten persons in a half cubic meter space?

Answer: The four million people gassed in Auschwitz are proof of it...

Question: When you say, they took 17 tons of gold from the corpses, are you basing that on a tonne of 1,000 kg?

Answer: Yes.

Question: Then do you also maintain that every victim, whether man, woman, child or baby, would have 4 grams of gold in his mouth?

91

> *Answer: It must have been that some had more and others less or even none; it would depend on the condition of their teeth."*

This is what Giant Hilberg calls a believable witness! How can any serious academic accept Hilberg's volumes when Hilberg offers such unbelievable testimony instead of physical or documentary evidence?

GITTA SERENY:

Author of *Into that Darkness* (published in German in 1980 by Ullstein with the title *Am Abgrund. Eine Gewissensforschung*). Hilberg refers to this book eight times.[164] The Hungarian Jewess G. Sereny interviewed former Treblinka commandant Franz Stangl many times as he sat in a Federal German prison, where, according to her book, he confirmed the mass murder in that camp. Shortly after their last conversation, Stangl died under mysterious circumstances. G. Sereny's work is completely worthless as a historical source because she does not provide any proof that Stangl actually made the statements attributed to him. She offers no tape recordings as evidence of the conversations, and she has not published any transcripts of her alleged interviews. Since a dead man cannot complain, Sereny can put into his mouth whatever she wants to.

In addition, even if Stangl had confessed to mass gassings in Treblinka, this would have been no proof. He had appealed from his sentence to life in prison, and to dispute the crime laid to him would have been interpreted as 'obdurate denial', which would preclude a reduction in the sentence or a pardon from the start. On the other hand, those accused who confessed could hope for some slight mercy from Federal German justice— as a reward for confirming the annihilation of the Jews.[165]

KURT GERSTEIN:

Main witness to mass gassings in Bełżec, was used by Hilberg as a source six times.[166] SS sanitation officer Gerstein described these gassings in a confession given after the war—or, better put, in six confessions, since, as Frenchman Henri Roques has shown, there are no less than six versions

---

164 Hilberg's footnotes 109, 113, 122, 194f., 501, 503f.; Hilberg's *DEJ* footnotes 10 (p. 896), 19 (p. 898), 93 (p. 916), 7 (p. 979), 10 (p. 980).

165 On the mechanisms employed in the course of the Federal German NS trials, see Wilhelm Stäglich, *Auschwitz. A Judge Looks at the Evidence*, 2nd ed., Institute for Historical Review, Costa Mesa, CA, 1990., 4th chapter; cf. also Manfred Köhler, *op. cit.* (note 114), pp. 85-131; on the Sereny book see also Arthur R. Butz, *"Context and Perspective in the 'Holocaust' Controversy"*, *The Journal of Historical Review* 3(4) (1982) pp. 371-405, (online: http://vho.org/GB/Journals/JHR/3/4/Butz371-405.html).

166 Hilberg's footnotes 88, 100, 380, 385, 463, 475; Hilberg's *DEJ* footnotes 86 (p. 890), 95, 98 (p. 892), 5 (p. 963), 10 (p. 964), 86 (p. 975), 98 (p. 976).

of the Gerstein confession, sometimes differing markedly from each other.[167] Gerstein killed himself in July 1945 in a French prison. He claimed that between 20 and 25 million people were gassed. He said that in Bełżec 700 to 800 Jews were stuffed into a gas chamber with a floor area of 25 m², which is 28 to 32 persons per square meter. Of Auschwitz, which he never entered, he affirmed that millions of children were killed by holding cotton wads soaked with hydrogen cyanide under their noses. Hallucinations about 35 to 40 m (115 to 130 ft) high piles of clothes and shoes of murdered prisoners top off this confession appropriately.[168]

RUDOLF REDER:

Next to Gerstein, Reder is the only witness to gassings in Bełżec and author of a book published in Cracow in 1946 on his experiences in that camp.[169] Hilberg cites him as a source twice.[170] Although he was over 60 at the time he was interned and there were certainly younger Jews available, he was chosen for the labor kommando. He lived for months on end under *"merciless monsters who commit horrible cruelties with sadistic delight"* and survived no less than 80 liquidation operations. One day the merciless monsters sent Reder and an SS man in a motor car on a shopping trip. The SS man went to sleep and Reder was able to escape.[171] In his report he claims that *three million people* were murdered in Bełżec.[172] The killing weapon he mentions is not a diesel motor, as Gerstein had said, but a gasoline motor.[173]

YANKIEL WIERNIK:

Polish Jew, shoemaker by trade and former Treblinka prisoner. He serves Hilberg as a source five times.[174] Here are two choice samples from his 'report of experiences':[175]

> *"The Ukrainians were constantly drunk, and sold everything they managed to steal in the camps in order to get more money for brandy. […] When they had eaten and drunk their fill, the Ukrainians looked around for*

---

167 *The "Confessions" of Kurt Gerstein*, Institute for Historical Review, Costa Mesa, CA, 1989.
168 The most detailed analysis of the Gerstein confessions is in Carlo Mattogno, *Il rapporto Gerstein. Anatomia di un falso*, Sentinella d'Italia, Monfalcone 1985.
169 Rudolf Reder, *op. cit.* (note 126).
170 Hilberg's footnotes 433, 435; Hilberg's *DEJ* footnotes 56, 58 (p. 971).
171 Rudolf Reder, *op. cit.* (note 126), p. 64.
172 N. Blumenthal (ed.), *Dokumenty i materialy*, v. I, p. 223, Łódź 1946.
173 Rudolf Reder, *op. cit.* (note 126), p. 44.
174 Hilberg's footnotes 44, 194, 440f., 462; Hilberg's *DEJ* footnotes 43 (p. 879), 91 (p. 916), 64 (p. 972), 85 (p. 974).
175 Alexander Donat, *op. cit.* (note 137), pp. 165, 170f.

other amusements. They frequently selected the best-looking Jewish girls from the transports of nude women passing their quarters, dragged them into their barracks, raped them and then delivered them to the gas chambers. [...]

The corpses were soaked in gasoline. This entailed considerable expense and the results were inadequate; the male corpses simply would not burn. Whenever an airplane was sighted overhead, all work was stopped, the corpses were covered with foliage as camouflage against aerial observation. It was a terrifying sight, the most gruesome ever beheld by human eyes. When corpses of pregnant women were cremated, their bellies would burst open. The fetus would be exposed and could be seen burning inside the mother's womb. [...] The gangsters are standing near the ashes, shaking with satanic laughter. Their faces radiate a truly satanic satisfaction. They toasted the scene with brandy and with the choicest liquors, ate, caroused and had a great time warming themselves by the fire."

Wiernik, the only witness who claims to have participated in the annihilation operations directly for an extended period of time, can tell us amazing things about corpses that burn on their own:[176]

"It turned out that bodies of women burned more easily than those of men. Accordingly, the bodies of women were used for kindling the fires."

Well, these are the major witnesses presented to a modern, intelligent world by a Giant of a Professor at the University of Vermont, and the taxpayers may rightly wonder why he was retained for some thirty years to *teach* their impressionable children!

b. Hilberg's Favorite Jewish Witness: Filip Müller

We finish our parade of 'credible' witnesses with Filip Müller. This one, a Slovakian Jew, spent three years in Auschwitz and belonged to the *Sonderkommando* that was assigned to crematory duty. In 1979, a full 34 years after the end of the war, with the help of ghost writer Helmut Freitag, he wrote a book titled *Sonderbehandlung*,[177] which Hilberg cites as a source no less than twenty times,[178] only six times less than star witness Number One, Rudolf Höß. Honor those who deserve honor! We quote here several passages from this book on the 'Holocaust' which is so fundamental for Hilberg.

---

176 *Ibid.*, p. 170.
177 Published by Steinhausen, Frankfurt a.M. Translated into English with revisions as *Eyewitness Auschwitz*, Stein and Day, New York, 1979, hereafter called *EA*.
178 Cf. Hilberg's footnotes 61, 209, 417, 418, 443, 444, 445, 446, 449, 450, 451, 452, 470, 471, 472, 473, 488, 489, 491, 511; Hilberg's *DEJ* footnotes 60 (p. 883), 74 (p. 911), 42 (p. 970), 66, 67, 68, 69 (p. 972), 72, 73, 74 (p. 973), 93, 94, 95, 96 (p. 976), 111, 112 (p. 978), 17 (p. 982).

On his first day at work Müller is in the gas chamber in the main camp at Auschwitz I:

> "*A violent blow, accompanied by Stark yelling: 'Get a move on, Strip the stiffs!' galvanized me into action. Before me lay the corpse of a woman. With trembling hands and shaking all over I began to remove her stockings. [...] I longed for a moment of rest. I kept a watchful eye on Stark and waited for a chance to take a breather while he was not looking. My moment came when he went across to the cremation room. Out of the corner of my eye I noticed a half-open suit-case containing food. Pretending to be busy undressing a corpse with one hand, I ransacked the suit-case with the other. Keeping one eye on the door in case Stark returned suddenly I hastily grabbed a few triangles of cheese and a poppy seed cake. With my filthy, blood-stained fingers I broke off pieces of cake and devoured them ravenously.*" (Müller, pp. 23f.; EA, p. 12)

What Müller describes here is a radical impossibility: He ate in a room polluted with hydrogen cyanide, which he could hardly have done with a gas mask on. Did the SS then make the crew of the *Sonderkommando* go into the gas chamber *without gas masks*—were they all somehow hydrogen cyanide-proof?

Obviously, in any hypothetical gassing of persons the victims should be made to undress beforehand; to have to take the clothes off the bodies would have complicated the procedure by adding hundreds of hours of tedious work and would have been an additional danger for the *Sonderkommando*, because hydrogen cyanide is poisonous on contact and can be absorbed by the skin.

> "*The powers that be had allocated twenty minutes for the cremation of three corpses.* [in one muffle] *It was Stark's duty to see to it that this time was strictly adhered to.*" (Müller, p. 20; EA, p. 16)

At the present day, the incineration of a corpse in the muffle of a modern crematory lasts nearly an hour on average.[179] That this applied as well to the crematories installed in the German concentration camps during wartime by the Topf firm, is shown by, among other things, the data for the Dutch transfer camp Westerbork, where the specified time period was strictly adhered to for every cremation.[180] If one were to cremate two corpses in one muffle—which is not provided for—one would approximately double the time needed, just as it takes approximately twice as long to burn a piece of wood weighing 2 kg in an oven than to burn a piece of

---

179 Verbal communication of Hans Häfeli, employee of the Basle crematorium, with the author, 10th February 1993.
180 On this, cf. Carlo Mattogno's study *I forni crematori di Auschwitz-Birkenau*, Edizioni di Ar, Padua 1999.

95

wood weighing 1 kg. If it were even possible to fit three corpses into one muffle, the incineration period would last nearly three hours, about twelve times longer than the time given by Müller. But no, "*the powers that be had allocated twenty minutes for the cremation of three corpses. It was Stark's duty to see to it that this time was strictly adhered to.*" Apparently, at the command of the SS even the Laws of Thermodynamics could be suspended.

Müller's impression of the German medical doctors was not especially favorable:

> "*From time to time SS doctors visited the crematorium, above all Hauptsturmführer Kitt and Obersturmführer Weber. During their visits it was just like working in a slaughterhouse. Like cattle dealers they felt the thighs and calves of men and women who were still alive and selected what they called the best pieces before the victims were executed. After their execution the chosen bodies were laid on a table. The doctors proceeded to cut pieces of still warm flesh from thighs and calves and threw them into waiting receptacles. The muscles of those who had been shot were still working and contracting, making the bucket jump about.*" (Müller, p. 74; EA, p. 46)

Müller decided to kill himself and join the condemned in the gas chambers, but:

> "*Suddenly a few girls, naked and in the full bloom of youth, came up to me. They stood in front of me without a word, gazing at me deep in thought and shaking their heads uncomprehendingly. At last one of them plucked up courage and spoke to me: 'We understand that you have chosen to die with us of your own free will, and we have come to tell you that we think your decision pointless: for it helps no one.' […] Before I could make an answer to her spirited speech, the girls took hold of me and dragged me protesting to the door of the gas chamber. There they gave me a last push which made me land bang in the middle of the group of SS men.*" (Müller, pp. 179f.; EA, p. 113f.)

Elsewhere, the Giant Professor Hilberg told his gullible readers that Jews were crowded into the gas chambers so tightly that children were thrown on top of their heads! But now, Hilberg presents eyewitness testimony alleging enough room for running and pushing the 'hero'. And what is worse: If the people in the chamber really knew what was about to happen, how can one expect them to push Müller out of an obviously open door, but not to try to escape themselves?

In summer 1944, when the Hungarian transports came to Birkenau, the *Sonderkommando* was kept busy:

> "*[…] the two pits were 40 to 50 meters long, about 8 meters wide and 2 meters deep. However, this particular place of torment was not yet ready for use by any means. Once the rough work was finished, there followed the realization of the refinements thought up by the arch-extermina-*

tor's warped ingenuity. Together with his assistant, Eckardt, [Hauptscharführer Otto Moll] *climbed down into the pit and marked out a 25 centimeters by 30 centimeters wide strip, running lengthways down the middle from end to end. By digging a channel which sloped slightly to either side from the center point, it would be possible to catch the fat exuding from the corpses as they were burning in the pit, in two collecting pans at either end of the channel.* [...]

    As the heap of bodies settled, no air was able to get in from outside. This meant that we stokers had constantly to pour petrol or wood alcohol on the burning corpses, in addition to human fat, large quantities of which had collected and was boiling in the two collecting pans on either side of the pit. The sizzling fat was scooped out with buckets on a long curved rod and poured all over the pit causing flames to leap up amid much crackling and hissing." (Müller, pp. 207f., 217f.; *EA*, pp. 130, 136)

Hilberg snatches up this outlandish nonsense on p. 1046 (*DEJ*, p. 978)! It is obvious that during cremations fat is the first thing to burn; it would never run down into troughs, but burst into flames wherever it appears, since liquid fat burnes like oil.

That the incinerations in the pits in Birkenau described by Müller—and other witnesses—could not have occurred in the time period in question is shown by photographs from the Allied aerial reconnaissance collections, whose interpretation is due mostly to extensive work by John Ball.[181] On a photograph from May 31, 1944, there are small clouds of smoke rising behind Crematory V which could never have come from an incineration of the size described. In all other locations and in all other photographs nothing of the kind can be seen.[182]

Müller says SS-Hauptscharführer Moll amused himself as follows:

    "Another unusual entertainment in which he would indulge every now and then was called swim-frog. The unfortunate victims were forced into one of the pools near the crematoria where they had to swim around croaking like frogs until they drowned from exhaustion." (Müller, p. 228; *EA*, p. 142)

Well, this is Filip Müller, Raul Hilberg's favorite Jewish witness, cited twenty times!—Perhaps Hilberg did not notice the following confession on p. 271 (*EA*, na) of Müller's master work:

    "[...] and I was not sure I had not dreamed the whole thing."

---

181 John C. Ball, *op. cit.* (note 53), pp. 235-248.
182 *Ibid.*, p. 247.

5. Hilberg's Description of the Annihilation of the Jews in the Light of Technology and Toxicology

The question, whether the things his witnesses describe are even possible technically and natural scientifically, does not occupy a second of Hilberg's time: What the witnesses said sounds right, and that's good enough. For obvious reasons these questions have been raised only by Revisionists.[183] We discuss them here first with respect to the 'pure extermination camps' and then for Auschwitz.

a. Diesel Motors as a Killing Weapon

Hilberg says that the murders were committed with diesel motors in Bełżec and Treblinka and that the Saurer trucks used for killing persons in Chełmno were also equipped with diesel motors. Hilberg claims 1.45 million Jews were killed by this method (750,000 in Treblinka, 550,000 in Bełżec and 150,000 in Chełmno).

The suitability of diesel exhaust gas for purposes of mass murder has been addressed most thoroughly by German-American engineer Friedrich P. Berg,[57] whose analysis we summarize here briefly:

While it is not in principle impossible to kill people with diesel exhaust gas, it is very difficult, since the latter contains very little poisonous carbon monoxide. While with a gasoline motor one can easily achieve a concentration of carbon monoxide of seven percent or more per cubic meter of air, with a diesel motor one cannot produce a concentration of carbon monoxide of even one percent. Experiments on animals have shown that it is impossible to kill the occupants of a diesel-fed gas chamber within the half hour claimed by the witnesses.[184] It would take at least three hours, and the motor would have to be run constantly under a heavy load.[185] In these circumstances, the fact that the motor might break down several times a day would also have to be taken into account.[186] This in turn means the motor

---

183 The only supporter of the theory of the annihilation of the Jews who has studied the technical aspects of the 'Holocaust' is Jean-Claude Pressac, but his analysis is technically unsound; on this cf. Robert Faurisson, "*Auschwitz : Technique and Operation of the Gas Chambers ou Bricolage et 'gazouillages' à Auschwitz et à Birkenau selon J.C. Pressac*", *Revue d'Histoire Révisionniste* 3 (1990/91), pp. 65-154 (online: http://vho.org/F/j/RHR/3/Faurisson65-154.html); Robert Faurisson, "*Antwort an Jean-Claude Pressac*", in: Herbert Verbeke (ed.), *op. cit.* (note 118), pp. 51-99 (online: http//vho.org/D/anf/Faurisson.html; Engl.: http://vho.org/GB/Books/anf/Faurisson1.html); Carlo Mattogno, "*Auschwitz. The Ende of a Legend*", Granata, Palos Verdes, CA, 1994 (online: http//vho.org/GB/Books/anf/Mattogno.html); Robert Faurisson, "*Procès Faurisson*", in: Robert Faurisson, *Écrits révisionnistes*, v. 4, privately published, Vichy 1999, pp. 1674-1682.
184 Kurt Gerstein claims it was 32 minutes before all victims were dead.
185 Simulated by artificial restriction of air flow.
186 The heavy accumulation of soot destroys the piston rings.

would have to be overhauled frequently—while the lines of the condemned lengthened outside the gas chamber.

The relative innocuousness of diesel motor exhaust is well known. It was for this reason that only diesel motors were allowed in the tunnel being built between England and France. If the Germans actually succeeded in murdering millions of Jews in record time and in disposing of their corpses without a trace, they were technical geniuses—but no technical genius would resort to a highly inefficient killing weapon.

The gasoline motor which Hilberg says was installed in Sobibór would have done better as a killing weapon. However, in 1991 the *Enzyklopädie des Holocaust* stated that the killing weapon in Sobibór was a diesel motor. Perhaps Hilberg and the *Enzyklopädie* will soon drop both the gasoline motor and the diesel motor and decide that the 200,000 to 250,000 murders in Sobibór were committed with "*a spirally, black substance dripping through holes in the ceiling*", as the persuasive Soviet-Jewish witness Alexander Pechersky stated in 1946. At that time, at least, 'memories' were still fresh.

b. Removal of Corpses in the 'Pure Extermination Camps': Case Study Bełżec

A principle of criminology is: Without a body there has been no murder! This rule is held to except where it can be proven that a body has been completely obliterated. Where then, are the corpses of the 1.65 million persons gassed in the 'pure extermination camps'? Where are the remains of the gigantic open air incinerations?

We are told that the 1.65 million dead were first buried in mass graves and later disinterred and incinerated. If these mass graves ever existed, the earth displacements caused by making them should still be distinguishable. Especially, they should be easily identifiable with aerial photography, due to altered topography and vegetation. Air photo expert John Ball has demonstrated how the aerial photography over Treblinka, Bełżec and Sobibór in 1944 shows no trace of large-scale movements of earth—which compels one to the conclusion that the gigantic mass graves for the interment of hundreds of thousands of corpses were never there.[187]

Unlike Raul Hilberg, we have visited the sites—but for research, not for photo sessions—where the 'Holocaust' supposedly unfolded, including Bełżec.[188] The slightly sloping place on the grounds of the former camp

---

187 John C. Ball, *op. cit.* (note 53), pp. 237f.
188 Together with Carlo Mattogno on 21st June 1997.

where the mass grave supposedly lay is labelled. It is markedly higher than the site where the gas chamber supposedly stood. Apparently, the Germans arranged their mass murder operation such that they would have to haul 550,000 or more bodies uphill!

Let us examine the technical preconditions for the claimed incineration without a trace of 550,000 corpses in Bełżec. (With respect to the other 'extermination camps' the numbers should be modified in proportion to the claimed number of victims.) Hilberg says that between late fall 1942 and March 1943, or, in other words, within four to five months at most, 550,000 corpses of gassed Jews were incinerated in at first one, and then two, incineration areas. Because of the frequent rain and snowfall at that time of year, we assume that the incinerations would have required 300 kg of wood per corpse,[189] meaning the total quantity of wood required would have been 165,000 tons. As has already been mentioned in chapter IV, open air incineration leaves behind human ashes amounting to approximately 5% of body weight. If we assume the latter was 50 kg, since if this was a mass murder there must have been many children among the victims, one body would leave behind 2.5 kg ashes; thus there would have been (550,000 × 2.5 =) 1,375,000 kg or 1,375 metric tons of ashes. There also would have been wood ashes, whose quantity varies depending on the type of wood, but cannot be less than 3 kg per ton of wood,[190] so that in Bełżec there would have been at least 495 tons of it. All told, after the mass incinerations there would have been nearly 2,000 metric tons of ashes. In this there would have been countless bones and teeth.

Where did the wood come from? How far from the camp did the inmates have to walk or be transported to cut this enormous amount of wood? How many inmates were required? How many tree cutting saws? Wedges? Wagons or trucks? Horses? Meals in the distant forests? How many guards to keep the inmates from escaping? Where was the wood stacked and aged and protected from the frequent rain or snow? Was it split into small pieces for quick burning? Small cuts are better for green wood to be used right away. How were the Germans able to dispose of the huge piles of ashes and the millions of pieces of bone and teeth? How could the 550,000 corpses have been incinerated in the open without the inhabitants of the town of Bełżec, one kilometer distant, noticing it—the enormous

---

189 Arnulf Neumaier states, based on a newspaper report, that in India, where open air cremations are common even today, 306 kg are required, on average ("*The Treblinka Holocaust*", *op. cit.* (note 43), p. 490). In Poland in late fall and winter it would be even greater, but we will stay with 300 kg, so as not to be accused of exaggerating.
190 *Ibid.*, p. 371.

amount of black smoke and the smell of human flesh burning had to be quite noticeable—and reporting it to the resistance movement? The latter was kept closely informed of events occurring at the local level in Poland and provided the exile government in London with a ceaseless stream of reports on developments in the country.[191] They reported nothing about a huge fire at Bełżec burning for months—were their couriers blind?

c. Zyklon B as a Killing Weapon

For a hypothetical mass gassing of humans with the disinfestation agent Zyklon B, it should be kept in mind that at normal temperatures it takes two hours for the hydrogen cyanide to escape the carrier substance. This slow rate of evaporation of the product was intended by its developers. For one thing, it made it possible for the application crew to leave the disinfestation chamber safely after spreading out the poison.[192] For another, the slow emission of the gas meant that a high concentration of poison gas could be achieved for an extended period of time, even when the gassed space was not air-tight and leaked gas. In this way the gas could penetrate to the farthest corners of the gassed building and kill the parasites dwelling there.

Therefore, even given the existence of an effective ventilation system, the ventilation of a hypothetical Zyklon B killing gas chamber could not have been completed sooner than two hours after the Zyklon granules were poured out, and also the *Sonderkommando* would have had to wait a considerable time for the ventilation to complete before they could enter the chamber. This they could have done only when wearing gas masks. Also they would certainly have needed protective suits, because the clearing of rooms crammed full of corpses would be sweaty work, and dangerous because hydrogen cyanide is a contact poison which can be easily absorbed by moist skin.

The witness statements stand in irreconcilable contradiction to these requirements. If several millions of people were murdered in Auschwitz—and such numbers were given in almost all of the witness statements cited by Hilberg from the immediate post-war period, even if he will not mention it—the gassing must have been done quickly with high throughput. Let us look at what a few of Hilberg's witnesses say on this subject:

---

191 On this, see J. Graf and C. Mattogno, *op. cit.* (note 87), Chapter 7.
192 Wearing of gas masks was required during this procedure. NI-9912.

FILIP MÜLLER:[193]

> "Already the evening before [the digging of the pits] three transports at about four hour intervals had disappeared into Crematory V and were gassed. After the screaming, groaning and rattling had died down, the gas chambers were ventilated for a couple of minutes. Then the SS sent the prisoner kommandos inside to take out the bodies."

RUDOLF VRBA:[150]

> "But by eleven o'clock, just two hours late, a car drew up. Himmler and Hoess got out and chatted for a while to the senior officers present. [...] At last, however, everything was ready for action. A sharp command was given to the S.S. man on the roof. He opened a circular lid and dropped the pellets quickly onto the heads below him. [...] when everyone inside was dead, [Himmler] took a keen interest in the procedure that followed. Special elevators took the bodies to the crematorium, but the burning did not follow immediately. Gold teeth had to be removed. Hair, which was used to make the warheads of torpedoes watertight, had to be cut from the heads of the women. The bodies of wealthy Jews, noted early for their potential, had to be set aside for dissection in case any of them had been cunning enough to conceal jewelry—diamonds, perhaps—about their person. It was, indeed, a complicated business, but the new machinery worked smoothly under the hands of skilled operators. Himmler waited until the smoke began to thicken over the chimneys and then he glanced at his watch. It was one o'clock. Lunch time, in fact."

FILIP FRIEDMAN:[194]

> "The gas worked quickly. After three to five minutes no one was left alive. After the bodies were taken away, the room was aired and a new group of victims was led in. At this tempo the gas chambers could handle 4,000 to 5,000 persons per hour."

RUDOLF HÖSS:[195]

> "When I built the annihilation building in Auschwitz, I needed Zyklon B, a crystallized hydrogen cyanide, which we threw into the death chamber through a small opening. It took 3 to 15 minutes, depending on climatic conditions, to kill the people in the death chamber. We knew when the people were dead, because their screaming stopped. We usually waited a half hour before we opened the doors and took away the bodies."

---

193 Filip Müller, *op. cit.* (note 177), p. 215 (*EA*, na).
194 F. Friedman, *op. cit.* (note 141), p. 54.
195 PS-3868.

CHARLES SIGISMUND BENDEL:[196]

> *"With blows from different kinds of sticks they were forced to go in and stay there, because when they realized that they were going to their death they tried to come out again. Finally, they* [the SS] *succeeded in locking the doors. One heard cries and shouts, and they started to fight against each other, knocking on the walls. This went on for two minutes and then there was complete silence. Five minutes later the doors were opened, but it was quite impossible to go in for another twenty minutes. Then the Special Kommandos started work."*

We recapitulate:

- Müller says the gas chambers were ventilated *"for a couple of minutes"* before the *Sonderkommando* crew went in.
- Vrba says that the gassing began around eleven o'clock; after the victims were dead their gold teeth were pulled, their hair cut off, and the *"wealthy Jews, noted early for their potential"* (so that one could find them without their clothes on among 3,000 corpses), were dissected. Two hours after they started, the whole operation is over, and Himmler can drive off to lunch!
- Friedman says that the gas chambers could handle 4,000 to 5,000 victims *per hour*. Within this time, therefore, the gassing process, the ventilation and the clearing of the chamber all took place!
- Höß says they waited for *"a half hour"* after the death of those shut inside, before they cleared the gas chamber.
- Bendel says the doors were opened five minutes after the victims had died, and the chamber was ventilated (into the corridor, where the hydrogen cyanide-proof SS men and *Sonderkommando* crew waited!). Then they waited another twenty minutes before the *Sonderkommando* stormed into the gas chamber.

In other words, what the witnesses say is not consistent with ordinary science and life's normal experiences! Yet, Hilberg is a 'true believer'.

The picture is completed by the analyses—which appeared after the *"definitive"* Hilberg edition came out—undertaken by Fred Leuchter[197] and Germar Rudolf[198] on mortar samples taken from the walls of the rooms in

---

196 *Trial of Josef Kramer and 44 others (The Belsen Trial)*, William Hodge and Company, London/Edinburgh/Glasgow 1949, p. 132.

197 Fred A. Leuchter, *An Engineering Report on the alleged Execution Gas Chambers at Auschwitz, Birkenau and Majdanek, Poland*, Samisdat Publishers, Toronto 1995. (online: http://www.zundelsite.org/english/leuchter/report1/leuchter.toc.htm). This work has its weaknesses, but since it is the first forensic study of this subject, it deserves to be mentioned.

198 Germar Rudolf, *The Rudolf Report*, Theses & Dissertations Press, Capshaw, AL, 2001, (online: http://vho.org/GB/Books/trr).

Birkenau identified as containing the alleged homicidal gas chambers. In contrast to the samples from the disinfestation chambers, they showed no significant concentrations of cyanide.

d. The Practical Course of the Gassings in Crematories II and III in Birkenau, as Told by Hilberg

Hilberg recapitulates the witness testimony briefly as follows:

> *"An SS man [...] lifted the glass shutter over the lattice and emptied one can after another into the gas chamber. [...] Within fifteen minutes (sometimes five), everyone in the gas chamber was dead.*
>
> *The gas was now allowed to escape and after about half an hour, the door was opened. [...] The Jewish work parties* (Sonderkommandos), *wearing gas masks, dragged out the bodies near the door to clear a path [...]"* (pp. 1042f.; *DEJ*, pp. 975f.)

On the size and holding capacity of the morgue cellars used as gas chambers he writes:

> *"The Leichenkeller were very large (250 square yards)* [200 m²]*, and 2,000 persons could be packed into each of them."* (p. 947; *DEJ*, p. 884)

The impossibility of the gassing process as described by the witnesses can be seen by examining the accompanying illustration.[199] Analysis of air-reconnaissance photographs from 1944, study of the original construction plans of the SS Central Construction Office in Auschwitz and architectural investigation of the present structures proves that there were no holes in the roof of the supposed gas chamber during the war. This led Professor Robert Faurisson to compose his now famous four-word motto:

No Holes? No 'Holocaust'!

Apart from the fact that the reported execution and ventilation periods are technically too brief and that there were no holes in the roofs of the 'gas chambers' (morgue I, marked no. 7 on the drawing)[200] the extermination method described here is absurd. The crews of the *Sonderkommando* were presented with a room crammed full of corpses (2,000 corpses in 200 m² means there were ten corpses per m²!), and now they faced the task of hauling them upstairs to the oven room. This they did with a elevator, which could hold at most 10 corpses at one time, which means it must have had to

---

199 John C. Ball, *The Ball Report*, Ball Resource Services, Delta, o.D., Drawing 7, p. 7. Prof. Dr. Robert van Pelt has published a drawing which is much better from an architectural standpoint (in: Robert van Pelt, Deborah Dwork, *Auschwitz: 1270 to the Present*, Yale University Press, New Haven and London 1996, p. 270). However, it has the critical defect that the draftswoman, Kate Mullin, has *fraudulently* added the ominous Zyklon B filling columns on Morgue Cellar 1, most likely at the direction of Prof. van Pelt. For this reason we do not show it here.

200 For the details see G. Rudolf, *op. cit.* (note 198).

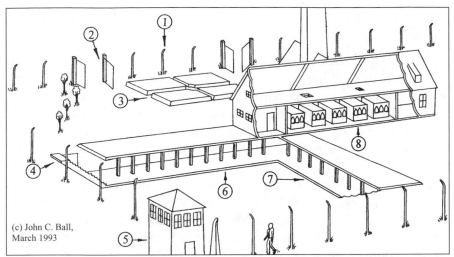

Cross-sectional drawing of Crematory II in Auschwitz-Birkenau, based on documentary construction plans, air-reconnaissance photographs and investigations of the present structures.

1. *Fence posts;*
2. *Open gate;*
3. *Garden;*
4. *Access stairway to Morgue Cellar 2;*
5. *Watch tower;*
6. *Morgue II, supposed undressing room;*
7. *Morgue I, supposed killing gas chamber with holes in the roof for introduction of Zyklon B—**the holes are not there!!!**;*
8. *5 ovens (three muffles each)*

rise and fall between the oven room and the gas chamber around 200 times per gassing. If each of the 15 muffles cremated one corpse per hour, after 24 hours there would still be (2,000 minus 360 =) 1,640 dead in the gas chamber—and now the next 2,000 would be coming in, since if the whole thing took place in spring or summer 1944, there were approximately 10,000 Jews gassed daily among the four crematories! How did the SS put these 2,000 Jews into a gas chamber containing 1,640 bodies from the day before?[201]

Raul Hilberg has studied many witness statements. Using them he has constructed a grotesque scheme of mass extermination in 'extermination camps', without pausing for a moment to wonder whether the whole thing could have happened that way at all. He is, to quote Robert Faurisson again, a "*paper historian*" who lives far from the physical reality of science and credible evidence.

---

201 Prof. Robert Faurisson was the first to point out to me the absurdity of the claimed gassing procedure (conversation in Vichy, March 1992).

e. The Claimed Incineration of Sometimes 10,000 Corpses Daily in Birkenau

Indeed, as Hilberg states on p. 946 (*DEJ*, p. 884), the four crematories in Birkenau put into operation from March 1943 possessed 46 firing chambers in all (15 each in Crematories II and III, 8 each in Crematories IV and V). The cremation of one corpse in a muffle takes, as has already been mentioned, on average one hour. Considering the fact that a coke-burning oven such as installed by the Topf firm in Birkenau cannot be operated continuously twenty-four hours a day, day in and day out—it must be cleaned regularly, and it needs to cool off before being cleaned—we assume a twenty hour period of operation, and even that is probably too high. In that case the 46 muffles at Birkenau had a maximum daily capacity of 920 corpses per day (20×46); we round this off to 1,000, to allow for the presence of children's corpses.

In view of these plain facts, the document cited by Hilberg on p. 1045 (*DEJ*, p. 978), supposedly a letter dated 28th June 1943 from the Central Construction Office at Auschwitz, in which the daily throughput for Crematories II and III was put at 1,440 each and for Crematories IV and V at 768 each, is certainly a forgery—probably of Soviet origin.[202] (*DEJ* has an error, giving as capacity of Crematories IV and V 268 each instead of 768.) Even in the Third Reich, technically impossible things did not happen.

Because the existence of the incineration pits reported by Filip Müller and other witnesses is refuted by the air-reconnaissance photographs, the incineration capacity claimed by Hilberg (10,000 corpses or more per day) is greater than the theoretical maximum possible by a factor of ten—and as a practical matter very much more, since we know from the investigations of Mattogno/Deana and Pressac that the crematories were noted for their frequent breakdowns, which would reduce their capacity drastically.

The only possible scientific conclusion is that the supposed many hundred thousand-fold murder of Jews in spring and fall 1944 could not have happened, because cremations of this quantity were technically impossible. Bodies do not generally disappear all on their own, even in the Third Reich.

---

202 On this cf. Manfred Gerner, "*Schlüsseldokument ist Fälschung*", *VffG*, 2(3) (1998), pp. 166-174 (online: http://vho.org/VffG/1998/3/Gerner3.html); cf. C. Mattogno, "*'Schlüsseldokument' – eine alternative Interpretation*", *VffG*, 4(1) (2000), pp. 51-56 (online: http://vho.org/VffG/2000/1/Mattogno51-56.html; Engl.: http://www.russgranata.com/lalett.html).

VIII. Hilberg's Statistics on Jewish Victims: Anatomy of Another Fraud

1. The 'Three Categories of Victims'

In his third volume, Hilberg discusses the Jewish population losses in the areas under German rule (pp. 1280-1300; *DEJ*, pp. 1199-1220). The relevant subchapter is entitled *"Statistics of Killed Jews"*, although 'Statistics of Deaths of Jews' would be more precise, because the statistics also include Jews who died in the camps and ghettos from epidemics, exhaustion and other causes. (In *DEJ* this subject is put in an appendix, entitled *"Statistics of Jewish Dead."*) Hilberg counts 5.1 million Jewish victims (p. 1300; *DEJ*, p. 1220) and misses the classical number six million by almost a million. On p. 1282 (*DEJ*, p. 1202) he writes:

> *"Any assessment based on additions must reflect the origins and meanings of the numbers found in wartime documents. The large majority of these figures stems from an actual count of the victims. By and large, the numbers fall into three categories: deaths as a result of (1) privation, principally hunger and disease in ghettos, (2) shootings, and (3) deportations to death camps."*

That the victim counts Hilberg postulates *"reflect... numbers found in wartime documents"*, of which *"the large majority... stems from an actual count"*, is, as we have said several times, pure flimflam.

On p. 1299 (*DEJ*, p. 1219) Hilberg identifies how victims in these three categories met their deaths. Here is his table in simplified form:

Death camps:	2,700,000 dead or less
Camps with low death counts, including labor and transit camps:	150,000 dead
Romanian and Croatian camps:	150,000 dead or less
Ghettos including Theresienstadt and privation outside ghettos:	800,000 dead or more
Open-air shootings (USSR, Serbia and *"elsewhere"*):	1,300,000 dead
TOTAL APPROXIMATELY:	5,100,000 DEAD

First, on the victims of open-air shootings; because of the insignificant number of Serbian Jews we restrict ourselves to the Soviet Union.

On pp. 409f. (*DEJ*, p. 390) Hilberg has attributed shootings of more than 900,000 Soviet Jews to the Einsatzgruppen, and adds, these correspond to *"only about two-thirds of the total number of Jewish victims in mobile operations"*. Therefore, 1.35 million Soviet Jews must have been killed. On p. 1300 (*DEJ*, p. 1220) he gives a far smaller number; he counts the number of Jewish victims in the Soviet Union as *"over 700,000"*, of which *"up to 130,000"* were in Lithuania, 70,000 were in Latvia and *"over 1,000"* were in Estonia (in *DEJ*, 2,000); given these statistics, the number of Jews killed in the territories of the Soviet Union, including the Baltic area can hardly have exceeded 900,000. What accounts for the difference of 450,000 as compared to the earlier number?

Possibly Hilberg has lumped in the Jews who fled from west to east in Poland following the partition of Poland in fall 1939 who were overtaken and killed by the German army after 22nd June 1941 with the figure of 900,000 Soviet Jewish victims in the second set of statistics. If there were 450,000 of them, they should have been subtracted from the number of Polish Jewish victims, but on p. 1300 (*DEJ*, p. 1220) Hilberg says there were *"up to 3 million"* of the latter. Since, as he tells us, there were 3.351 million Jews in Poland in August 1939, shortly before the German invasion (p. 1288; *DEJ*, na), there cannot have been 3 million of these annihilated in Poland itself and 450,000 in the USSR if the Germans had exterminated all of Polish Jewry without exception.

So it is clear from the start that Hilberg is playing with marked cards.

Hilberg says the number of Jews who died in the 'common' concentration camps Dachau, Buchenwald, Mauthausen and Stutthof and also in work and transit camps was 150,000, which is in the realm of possibility.[203] We can say nothing on the victim count of 150,000 ascribed to Romanian and Croatian camps because we have not studied these camps.

There remain the 800,000 victims in the ghettos and those resulting from privation outside the ghettos. How in heaven's name does Hilberg arrive at this number? Most Polish Jews were supposedly fetched from the ghettos and transported to the 'extermination camps' and gassed there, and the Jews from the ghettos in the USSR were allegedly shot when the ghettos were broken up. Does Hilberg count these deaths twice? Apparently yes, because otherwise the desired final totals would never be reached!

---

203 In Poland there were hundreds of small work camps which were not considered outlying camps of the official concentration camps. An overview of these camps can be found in the work published by the Głowna Komisja Badania Zbrodni Hitlerowskich w Polsce (Head Commission for the Investigation of Hitler Crimes in Poland) entitled *Obozy Hitlerowskie na Ziemiach Polskich*, Panstwowe Wydawnictwo Naukowe, Warsaw 1979.

Over 2.5 million imaginary gassing victims, a massively inflated number of shooting victims, a massively inflated number of deaths in the ghettos and due to privation outside ghettos—by these means the 'Holocaust' pope sees to it that he can count, if not six, at least over five million dead Jews.

Let us examine Hilberg's statistics for three critical countries.

2. Hungary

In 1944 Hungarian Jews were indisputably visited with two great deportations. Between May and July most of the Jews living outside Budapest were deported, mostly to Auschwitz. According to the dispatches of the German special ambassador in Budapest, Edmund Veesenmayer, the number of deportees was 437,402. The operation was stopped on 7th July by Hungarian Regent Miklos Horthy and the Jews of Budapest were spared further deportation. In October, after the fall of Horthy and the seizure of power by Arrow Cross forces (Hungarian National Socialists) under Ferenc Szalasi, many thousand Hungarian Jews were driven to the borders of the Reich in forced marches to build fortifications against a Soviet invasion.

Of the first deportations the *Enzyklopädie des Holocaust* writes:[204]

> *"Most of the Hungarian Jews were gassed shortly after their arrival in Auschwitz-Birkenau."*

Hilberg also asserts (on p. 1000; *DEJ*, p. 936) that *"the great bulk"* of Hungarian deportees in 1944 *"were gassed in the Auschwitz killing center upon arrival"*. On the other hand, in a table on p. 1300 (*DEJ*, p. 1220) dealing with *"Deaths by Country"*, he gives the total number of Hungarian-Jewish victims as *"over 180,000"*. Because this must include the deaths from the second deportation, carried out in October 1944, then, of the 437,000 displaced between May and July, clearly less than 180,000 met their deaths and thus many more than half survived the war. Thereby Hilberg undercuts his own assertion that *"the great bulk"* was gassed. Where were people sent who did not die in Auschwitz? Hilberg mentions several thousand transferred elsewhere (pp. 999f.; *DEJ*, na). What happened to the others? The readers are never told.

Nor are they told where Hilberg has gotten his figure of 180,000 Hungarian-Jewish victims.

Because the claimed mass annihilation in Birkenau cannot have taken place due to its radical technical impossibility, it is likely that the actual

---

204 v. III, p. 1467.

population losses of Hungarian Jews did not exceed several tens of thousands. Auschwitz was probably a transit camp (*Durchgangslager*) for the Hungarian Jews who were not registered there. The proven transfers from Auschwitz to Stutthof[205] mesh with this description closely.

3. Poland

Someone not familiar with the difficulties of population statistics might think that the demographic losses of Jews in Poland could be determined by subtracting the number of Jews living there *after* the war from the number living there *before* the war. This is the method used in, among others, the collected work edited by the notorious Prof. Wolfgang Benz, *Dimension des Völkermords*,[206] in which the concept of Jewish emigration does not appear. Hilberg concedes magnanimously that 15,000 Polish Jews emigrated "*to Palestine and other areas*" during the war and that "*thousands*" survived in the territories annexed by the Soviet Union or were deported by the Soviets (p. 1293; *DEJ*, p. 1213). He says "*up to 3 million*" Polish Jews died (p. 1300; *DEJ*, p. 1220), which is almost 90% of the (claimed) 3.351 million alive before the war.

This three million number is a pure fantasy. For one thing, the starting number is too high, since the last Polish census before the war, according to which 3,113,033 Jews lived in Poland, took place in 1931 and, according to the Institute for Contemporary History in Munich, during the decade of the '30s some 100,000 Jews a year emigrated from Poland.[207] After Poland was partitioned in fall 1939 there was a massive flight of Jews out of the German half into the Soviet half. In his study *The Dissolution*, Sanning names numerous towns from which more than half the Jews had moved to the east. Although on 22nd June 1941 the Soviet occupied area of Poland came quickly under the control of the Wehrmacht, a large share of the Jews there fled with the Red Army and some had previously been deported further east by Stalin's willing executioners.

According to a report in the *United Press* in February 1946, 800,000 Jews still lived in Poland.[208] The following facts should also be noted:

– immediately after the end of the war numerous Polish Jews emigrated to America, Palestine and other places;

---

205 Cf. chapter VI.5.
206 Published 1991 by R. Oldenbourg.
207 Expert report of the Institute of Contemporary History, Munich 1958, cited by W. Sanning, *op. cit.* (note 33), p. 32.
208 *Keesings Archiv der Gegenwart*, 16th/17th year, Essen 1948, Reported on 15.2.1946.

- most Polish Jews who had fled to the USSR stayed there;
- many Polish Jews who remained in Poland after the war changed their names and became difficult to recognize as Jews.[209]

We do not possess reliable figures for this problem, so it is not possible to calculate Jewish population losses in Poland even approximately. In any case, of Hilberg's up to three million deaths, the imaginary gassing victims should be subtracted (most of the 1.65 exterminated in the 'pure extermination camps' and a substantial number of those killed in Auschwitz were supposedly Polish Jews). The probable magnitude of Jewish losses in Poland is up to several hundred thousand and truly a tragedy.

4. The Soviet Union

The census of 1939 showed 3.02 million Soviet Jews, but in 1940 the *American Jewish Yearbook*[210] reported that there were 5.5 million. This can only be explained if a large share of Polish, Baltic and Romanian Jewry were absorbed by the USSR. But, according to the census of 1959, 2.267 million Jews lived in Soviet lands. However, in the Soviet census every citizen could give the nationality that he thought he belonged to and large numbers of Soviet Jews had assimilated; the latter no longer regarded themselves as Jews, but as Russians, Ukrainians, and so on. In addition, a powerfully anti-Zionist mood was prevalent and an acknowledgement of being Jewish might have brought harassment with it.

Amazingly, however, on 1st July 1990—long after the beginning of emigration to Israel and to the USA—the *New York Post* referred again to five million Soviet Jews. Because of this unholy chaos of numbers, it is clear that it is not possible to come to a reliable estimate of the extent of Soviet-Jewish population losses in the Second World War—quite apart from the fact that one also must take account of Jewish members of the Red Army fallen in battle as well as Jewish civilians who died of starvation in areas that were not German occupied, whose deaths were not due to German persecution measures and had nothing to do with the 'Holocaust'.

5. Summary

Hilberg's figure of approximately 250,000 deaths of Jews in German concentration, work and transit camps—to be clearly distinguished from

---

209 On this, cf. for example, Jozef Pawlikowski, *"Einige Anmerkungen zu jüdischen Bevölkerungs-statistiken"*, VffG, 2(1) (1998), pp. 36f. (online: http://vho.org/VffG/1998/1/Pawlikowski.html)
210 1941, v. 43, p. 319.

'extermination camps'—is almost certainly too high, but it may be in the right range. Jews who died in Auschwitz and Majdanek of sickness, exhaustion and so on, should also be included in this number. Of the maximum 210,000 deaths incurred at these two camps,[211] some 60% were probably Jewish. This means that at most some 350,000 Jews could have met their deaths in German camps. The mass shootings in the Soviet Union, the misery in the ghettos and the evacuation of the camps in the last months of the war could not have cost more than several hundred thousand Jewish lives.

The final figure of Jewish population losses must be much less than one million.

This estimate is confirmed by the investigations of Swedish researcher Carl Nordling. Based on the biographical data of the first 722 Jewish personalities listed in the *Encyclopaedia Judaica* in 1972 who lived in their European homelands when the war began, he determined that of these, 44% emigrated, 35% remained in their homelands but were spared deportations or internment, 8% were deported but survived and 13% died.[212]

In his study based exclusively on Jewish and Allied statistics, W. Sanning comes to the conclusion that not more than 3.5 million Jews were subject to German power, meaning that they lived in the German area of influence at the time when the 'Holocaust' was supposedly transpiring.[213] Let us assume that Sanning's number is too low and that the number of Jews living in the German area of control was 5 million. Let us also assume that Nordling's statistics are not representative and that not 13%, but 20% of Jews died in the German area of control. In this case, the number of Jewish victims would run to one million—only a fifth of Hilberg's 'calculated' or invented number.

Hilberg's methods can be quite clearly seen in his treatment of the demographically key country Poland. He ignores the massive emigration of Jews out of Poland before the war, plays down the mass flight of Polish Jews into the USSR in 1939, lets innumerable 'victims of gassing in the extermination camps' die a second time as 'killed in shootings behind the eastern front' or 'perished in the ghettos', does not bother to mention the many hundreds of thousands of Polish Jews who emigrated after the war and pays no attention to the fact that many Polish Jews were no longer recognized as such after 1945. One could not shift and chop statistics any more dishonestly than our Giant has done!

---

211 Cf. notes 106 and 107 in chapter VII.2.
212 *Revue d'Histoire Révisionniste*, 2 (1990), pp. 50-64 (http://vho.org/F/j/RHR/2/Nordling50-64.html).
213 W. Sanning, *op. cit.* (note 33), p. 181.

IX. Hilberg's Debacle at the First Zündel Trial

In Toronto in 1985, a trial took place against the German-Canadian Ernst Zündel. At the instigation of a *"Holocaust Remembrance Association"* he had been accused of breaking a law against *"spreading false news"*—which was later declared by Canada's Supreme Court to be unconstitutional—because he had distributed Richard Harwood's pamphlet *Did Six Million Really Die?* The trial ended with Zündel sentenced to a 15 months prison term. The sentence was reaffirmed by a trial on appeal—in 1988—but the term of imprisonment was reduced to 9 months, and on August 27, 1992, the Canadian Supreme Court threw out the conviction.

Raul Hilberg had been called in the first trial as a witness for the prosecution. Mercilessly pressed by Zündel's combative attorney Douglas Christie, to whom Robert Faurisson, present in the courtroom, frequently passed notes with pertinent questions, the Giant of the *"standard work"* on the 'Holocaust' met his Waterloo. He rejected an invitation to testify at the trial on appeal three years later, but prosecutor Peter Griffiths requested that his statements given in the initial trial three years before be read again in court.

In her excellent narrative *Did Six Million Really Die?*—bearing the same title as the Harwood pamphlet that had led to the trial—Barbara Kulaszka has partially summarized Hilberg's statements and partially quoted them directly from the transcript of the trial.

Christie asked Hilberg about the Hitler order for the extermination of all Jews which had appeared in his first edition (the second edition was then in preparation). After endless excuses, Hilberg finally conceded that there was no proof for such an order.[214]

Later the following exchange occurred between Christie and Hilberg:[215]

"'What do you mean by a scientific report?,' asked Hilberg.

---

214 Barbara Kulaszka, *op. cit.* (note 1), pp. 22-25.
215 *Ibid.*, p. 39.

Raul Hilberg during the Zündel trial in Toronto 1985

I don't usually have to define simple words, said Christie, but by 'scientific report' I mean a report conducted by anyone who purported to be a scientist and who examined physical evidence. Name one report of such a kind that showed the existence of gas chambers anywhere in Nazi-occupied territory. (5-968)

'I still don't quite understand the import of your question,' said Hilberg. 'Are you referring to a German, or a post-war—'

I don't care who—German, post-war, Allied, Soviet—any source at all. Name one, said Christie.

'To prove what?,' asked Hilberg.

To conclude that they have physically seen a gas chamber. One scientific report, repeated Christie.

'I am really at a loss. I am very seldom at such a loss, but... [...]

Judge Locke interrupted: 'Doctor... do you know of such a report?'

'No,' replied Hilberg."

With respect to Kurt Gerstein, who is quoted as a source in his book a number of times, Christie asked Hilberg whether he would not normally consider someone to be crazy or a liar who maintained that one could stuff between 28 and 32 persons per square meter in a room 1.8 m high:[216]

"'Well, on this particular datum I would be very careful,' said Hilberg, 'because Gerstein, apparently, was a very excitable person. He was capable of all kinds of statements [...]

Christie produced the Gerstein statement and proceeded to ask Hilberg whether certain statements appeared in the statement. Hilberg agreed that in his statement, Gerstein alleged that 700-800 persons were crushed

---

216 *Ibid.*, pp. 31ff.

together in 25 square metres in 45 cubic metres; he also agreed that he had ignored this part of Gerstein's statement in his book. [...]

And he refers to Hitler and Himmler witnessing gassings, right?, asked Christie.

Hilberg agreed that Gerstein had made this statement and that it was 'absolutely' and 'totally' false [...]

Christie asked Hilberg whether he considered Gerstein's statement— that at Bełżec and Treblinka nobody bothered to make a count and that in fact about 25 million people, not only Jews, were actually killed—was credible?

'Well, parts of it are true, and other parts of it are sheer exaggeration, manifest and obvious exaggeration. To me, the important point made in this statement is that there were no counting at the point at which people entered the gas chamber,' said Hilberg.

So you take the obviously exaggerated part out and use the part that you thought was credible, that there was no counting. Right?, asked Christie.

'Yes.'"

Hilberg had to admit that all the 'proofs' for mass murder in the eastern camps stemmed from Stalinist Soviet sources:[217]

"The whole site, suggested Christie, was within the Soviet sphere of control, and nobody from the west was allowed into those camps to investigate, isn't that right?

'Well, I don't know of any requests made to investigate... When you say no one was allowed, it implies some request,' said Hilberg. '... All I could say is, I know of no Western investigators early on in Auschwitz, or any of...' (5-1072)

Treblinka?, asked Christie.

'Well, there was no more Treblinka in 1945.'

Sobibór?

'That was no more.'

Majdanek?

'Majdanek is another matter.'

Was there anybody from the West that went to Majdanek?, asked Christie.

'Not to my knowledge.'

Bełżec?

---

217 *Ibid.*, p. 53.

> *'Bełżec was the first camp to have been obliterated.'*
> *Chełmno or Stutthof?*
> *'No, sir.'*
> *Auschwitz or Birkenau?*
> *'No.'"*

Concerning Rudolf Höß, Hilberg's star witness for the mass murder at Auschwitz whom he cites many times, Christie asked why he had mentioned a non-existent camp, Wolzek:[218]

> *"'Yes, I have seen that garbled reference,' said Hilberg. 'It may have been Bełżec. It's very hard, if the man did not write anything, if he said things, if he was tired, if he was misunderstood, if he misspoke himself...'*
>
> *Christie pointed out that Höß referred to Bełżec as well as Wolzek.*
>
> *I suggest to you, he said to Hilberg, that there is a reason to believe that this man was not only being obliged to sign a confession in a language he didn't understand, but things were being put into a statement for him that were patently absurd, like Gerstein.*
>
> *'There was obvious confusion in this one statement,' said Hilberg.*
>
> *Christie produced Nuremberg document 3868-PS, the Höß affidavit. Hilberg agreed he had seen the document before and agreed he had seen the Wolzek reference. 'Yes, I've seen that reference. It's terrible.' (5-1076)*
>
> *It's obvious that something wasn't quite right about that individual, would you agree?, asked Christie.*
>
> *'No, I wouldn't say that something wasn't quite right about the individual,' said Hilberg. 'I would say that something wasn't quite right about the circumstances under which this was made as an affidavit. [...]"*

With the "*circumstances* [about which] *something wasn't quite right*", Hilberg undoubtedly meant the three days of torture with which the confession was wrung from Rudolf Höß whom he quotes twenty-six times as the star witness for the annihilation of the Jews.

---

218 *Ibid.*, p. 54.

X. Conclusions

During the Second World War the Jews in the countries of Europe controlled by Germany suffered massive persecutions and paid a high price in blood.

In a labor over forty years, Raul Hilberg has assembled an immense number of documents on these events. Based on these documents, he could have written a work entitled *The Persecution of the European Jews* (*Die Verfolgung der europäischen Juden*) that would have stood the test of time and earned him a name as a historian of the first rank.

Raul Hilberg has spoiled his chance. He wanted to document not only the *persecution* of the European Jews, but also, and mainly, the *destruction* of same, by which he meant mainly the industrialized mass murder in chemical slaughterhouses. He had a hidden agenda.

There is no tangible physical evidence of any such industrialized mass murder, and in the mountains of documents that have been saved from the war years there is not the least indication for such a horrendous charge. In order to 'prove' this mass murder, Hilberg has had to invert the long-standing hierarchy of evidence and make witness testimony take precedence over physical and documentary evidence. Instead of the latter, we have the testimony of a Rudolf Höß, who confessed to having visited in June 1941 the camp Treblinka, which only opened in July 1942, of a Kurt Gerstein, who maintains that in Bełżec one could squeeze 32 persons into a square meter, of a Filip Müller, who tells us that when corpses were incinerated the fat ran down in channels from which one could scoop it out with dippers.

In 1982, Hilberg responded to the Revisionists who had reproached him with faulty methodology with the following argument:[219]

> *"The critics cannot explain one very simple fact: What became of the people who were deported? The deportations were not kept secret. They were announced. Many millions of people were shipped to very specific places. Where are these people? They are certainly not hiding in China!"*

---

219 *Le Nouvel Observateur*, 3rd-9th July 1982, pp. 70 ff.

Indeed, where are these people? Hilberg is right that they are not hiding in China. Where they ended up is illustrated by an article on 24th November 1978 in the *State Times* (Baton Rouge, Louisiana, p. 8a):

> *"The Steinbergs once flourished in a small Jewish village in Poland. That was before Hitler's death camps. Now more than 200 far-flung survivors and descendants are gathered here to share a special four-day celebration that began, appropriately, on Thanksgiving day. Relatives came Thursday from Canada, France, England, Argentina, Columbia, Israel and at least 13 cities across the United States. 'It's fabulous', said Iris Krasnow of Chicago. 'There are five generations here—from 3 months old to 85. People are crying and having a wonderful time. It's almost like a World War II refugee reunion'."*

These are concrete examples of Hilberg's 'gassing victims'!

In a society which has chosen the lie as its *leitmotif*, Raul Hilberg is honored for his work. Yet his fame is built on sand, and he is a giant with feet of clay whose fall is only a question of time.

A fair judgment of Hilberg's work was unwittingly made by himself. In a letter to Dr. Robert H. Countess, the responsible publisher of this book, Prof. Raul Hilberg wrote:[220]

> *"Superficiality is the major disease in the field of Holocaust studies."*

When asked whether he once stated that there is no quality control in holocaust studies, he confirmed this in 2000:[221]

> *"That is correct, especially at several U.S. elite universities."*

And the University of Vermont, Hilberg's Alma Mater, is definitely one of them. Let us conclude with a passage from Robert Faurisson:[222]

> *"R. Hilberg's huge work is reminiscent of the erudite undertakings of bygone eras, when Christian, Jewish and Byzantine scholars competed with each other in the production of all kinds of literary or historical forgeries. Their knowledge excited admiration, but what they lacked was conscience. There is a striking similarity between R. Hilberg with his 'remarkable cabalistic mentality'—to borrow a phrase from A.R. Butz—and those Jews of Alexandria, who, Bernard Lazare tells us, 'expended an extraordinary amount of labor to forge the very texts which they used to support themselves in their fight for their cause'."*

---

220 Personal correspondence with R. H . Countess, June 21, 1988.
221 Eva Schweitzer, *"Rücksicht auf die Verbündeten"*, *Berliner Zeitung*, Sept. 4, 2000.
222 Robert Faurisson, *Écrits révisionnistes…*, *op. cit.* (note 3), p. 1895.

The Opponents

Raul Hilberg, born in Austria 1926, emigrated to the USA 1939, B.A. in political science, M.A. and Ph.D. in Public Law and Administration (1955). Instructor at the University of Vermont, later Professor of International Relations, US Foreign Policy, and the Holocaust.

Books: *The Destruction of the European Jews* (1961, 1985), *Die Vernichtung der europäischen Juden* (1982, 1997), *Documents of Destruction. Germany and Jewry, 1933-1945* (1971), *Sonderzüge nach Auschwitz* (1981), *The Holocaust Today* (1988), *Gehorsam oder Initiative? Zur arbeitsteiligen Täterschaft im Nationalsozialismus* (1991), *Perpetrators, Victims, Bystanders. The Jewish Catastrophe, 1933-1945* (1992), *Täter, Opfer, Zuschauer. Die Vernichtung der Juden 1933-1945* (1992), *Unerbetene Erinnerung: der Weg eines Holocaust-Forschers* (1994), *L'Insurrection du ghetto de Varsovie* (with others, 1994), *The Politics of Memory* (1996).

Jürgen Graf, born in Switzerland 1951, studied Scandinavian, English and Roman languages at the University of Basel, awarded degree of Magister; instructor by profession; for four years German instructor at Chinese Culture University, Taipei, Taiwan; Revisionist researcher and historian since 1991.

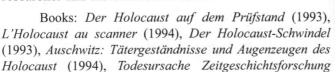

Books: *Der Holocaust auf dem Prüfstand* (1993), *L'Holocaust au scanner* (1994), *Der Holocaust-Schwindel* (1993), *Auschwitz: Tätergeständnisse und Augenzeugen des Holocaust* (1994), *Todesursache Zeitgeschichtsforschung* (1996), *Das Rotbuch. Vom Untergang der Schweizerischen Freiheit* (1997), *KL Majdanek. Eine historische und technische Studie* (with C. Mattogno, 1998), *Das KL Stutthof und seine Funktion in der nationalsozialistischen Judenpolitik* (with C. Mattogno, 1999), *Riese auf Tönernen Füßen. Raul Hilberg und sein Standardwerk über den 'Holocaust'* (1999), *The Giant With Feet of Clay. Raul Hilberg and his Standard Work on the 'Holocaust'* (2001), *Concentration Camp Stutthof and its Function in National Socialist Jewish Politics* (with C. Mattogno, 2001)

Sources

- *American Jewish Yearbook*, 1941, v. 43.
- Aroneanu, Eugène, *Camps de Concentration*, Office Français d'Edition, Paris 1945.
- Aronson, Gregor, *Soviet Russia and The Jews*, New York 1949.
- Aynat, Enrique, *Estudios sobre el "Holocausto"*, Gráficas Hurtado, Valencia 1994.
  - *Los protocolos de Auschwitz: ¿Una fuente histórica?*, Garcia Hispán, Alicante 1990.
- Bauer, Yehuda, *Canadian Jewish News,* 30th January 1992.
- Baynac, Jacques, *Le Nouveau Quotidien*, Lausanne, 3rd September 1997.
- Becker, Fritz, *Im Kampf um Europa*, Leopold Stocker Verlag, Graz/Stuttgart 1993.
  - *Stalins Blutspur durch Europa*, Arndt Verlag, Kiel 1996.
- Begunov, Juri K., *Tajnye Sily w Istorii Rossij*, Isdatelstwo Imeni A.S. Syborina, St. Petersburg 1996.
- Benz, Wolfgang, *Dimension des Völkermords*, R. Oldenbourg, 1991.
- Berben, Paul, *Dachau. The Official History*, The Norfolk Press, 1975.
- Black, Edwin, *The Transfer Agreement*, New York-London 1994.
- Blumenthal, N. (ed.), *Dokumenty i materiały*, Łódź 1946.
- Boog, Horst, and others, *Das Deutsche Reich und der Zweite Weltkrieg*, v. 4: *Der Angriff auf die Sowjetunion*, Deutsche Verlags-Anstalt, Stuttgart 1987.
- Broszat, Martin, *Die Zeit*, 19th August 1960.
- Browning, Christopher, *"The Revised Hilberg"*, in: *Simon Wiesenthal Center Annual*, 1986.
- Butler, Rupert, *Legions of Death*, Arrow Books, London 1983.
- Butz, Arthur R., *The Hoax of the Twentieth Century*, Institute for Historical Review, Newport Beach, Calif. 1976, 1992.
  - *"Context and Perspective in the 'Holocaust' Controversy"*, The Journal of Historical Review 3(4) (1982) pp. 371-405.
  - *"On the 1944 Deportations of Hungarian Jews"*, The Journal of Historical Review, 19(4) (July/August 2000), pp. 19-28.
- Colloque de l'Ecole des Hautes Etudes en sciences sociales, *L'Allemagne nazie et le génocide juif*, Gallimard-Le Seuil, Paris 1985.

- Czech, Danuta, *"Kalendarium der Ereignisse im Konzentrationslager Auschwitz-Birkenau"*, in: *Hefte von Auschwitz*, v. 2-4, 6-8 (1959-1964, 1st edition).

  - *Kalendarium der Ereignisse im Konzentrationslager Auschwitz-Birkenau 1939-1945*, Rowohlt, Reinbek 1989

  - *Auschwitz Chronicle: 1939-1945*, I.B. Tauris, London/New York 1990

- Dawidowicz, Lucy, *The War against the Jews*, Penguin Books, New York 1975.

- Donat, Alexander, *The Death Camp Treblinka*, Holocaust Library, New York 1979.

- Danuta Drywa, *"Ruch transportów między Stutthof i innymi obozami"*, in: *Stutthof. Zeszyty Muzeum*, no. 9, Stutthof 1990.

- Dunin-Wąsowicz, Krzysztof, *"Żydowscy Więźniowie KL Stutthof"*, in: *Biuletyn Żydowskiego Instytutu Historycznego*, no. 63, Warsaw 1967.

- Eichmann, Adolf, *Ich, Adolf Eichmann*, Druffel, Leoni 1980.

- Faurisson, Robert, *"Mon expérience du révisionnisme"*, in: *Annales d'Histoire Révisionniste*, no. 8, spring 1990.

  - *"Auschwitz : Technique and Operation of the Gas Chambers ou Bricolage et 'gazouillages' à Auschwitz et à Birkenau selon J.C. Pressac"*, *Revue d'Histoire Révisionniste* 3 (1990/91).

  - *Écrits révisionnistes (1974-1999)*, 4 vols., published by author, Vichy 1999.

- Friedman, Filip, *This Was Oswiecim*, The United Jewish Relief Appeal, London 1946.

- Gauss, Ernst (ed.), *Dissecting the Holocaust*, Theses & Dissertations Press, Capshaw, AL, 2000.

- Gerner, Manfred, *"Schlüsseldokument ist Fälschung"*, *Vierteljahreshefte für freie Geschichtsforschung*, 2(3) (1998), pp. 166-174.

- Głowna Komisja Badania Zbrodni Hitlerowskich w Polsce (ed.), *Obozy hitlerowskie na ziemiach polskich 1939-1945*, Panstwowe Wydawnictwo Naukowe, Warsaw 1979.

- Graf, Jürgen, *Auschwitz. Tätergeständnisse und Augenzeugen des Holocaust*, Neue Visionen, Würenlos 1994.

  - *Der Holocaust-Schwindel*, Guideon Burg Verlag, Basel 1993.

  - *"What Happened to the Jews Who Were Deported to Auschwitz but Were Not Registered There?"*, *The Journal of Historical Review*, 19(4) (2000), pp. 4-18.

  - and Carlo Mattogno, *Concentration Camp Stutthof and its Function in National Socialist Jewish Politics*, Theses & Dissertations Press, Capshaw, AL, 2001.

  - and Carlo Mattogno, *KL Majdanek*, Castle Hill Publishers, Hastings 1998.

- Grossman, Wassili, *Die Hölle von Treblinka*, Foreign Language Publication House, Moscow 1947.

- Hilberg, Raul, *The Destruction of the European Jews*, Quadrangle Books, Chicago 1967.

– *The Destruction of the European Jews*, 3 vols., Holmes and Meier Publishers, New York, 1985.
– *Die Vernichtung der europäischen Juden*, 3 vols., Fischer Taschenbuch Verlag, Frankfurt 1997.
– *Le Nouvel Observateur,* 3rd-9th July 1982, pp. 70ff.
– *Newsday,* 23rd February 1983, p. II/3.
– Hitler, Adolf, *Mein Kampf,* Franz Eher Verlag, Munich 1933.
– Hitler, Adolf, *Völkischer Beobachter,* 30th September 1942.
– Hoffmann, Joachim, "*Die Sowjetunion bis zum Vorabend des deutschen Angriffs*", in: Horst Boog and others, *Das Deutsche Reich und der Zweite Weltkrieg*, vol. 4: *Der Angriff auf die Sowjetunion*, Deutsche Verlags-Anstalt, Stuttgart 1987.
– *Stalin's War of Extermination*, Theses & Dissertations Press, Capshaw, AL, 2001.
– "*The Soviet Union's Offensive Preparations in 1941*", in: *From Peace to War.* Providence/Oxford, 1997, pp. 361-380.
– Höß, Rudolf, *Kommandant in Auschwitz*, edited by Martin Broszat, dtv, Munich 1983.
– International Military Tribunal, *Trial of the Major War Criminals*, 42 vols., Nuremberg 1947-1949.
– Jäckel, Eberhard, Peter Longerich, Julius H. Schoeps (eds.), *Enzyklopädie des Holocaust*, Argon Verlag, Berlin 1993.
– Jäckel, Eberhard, and Jürgen Rohwer, *Der Mord an den Juden im Zweiten Weltkrieg*, Deutsche Verlagsanstalt, Stuttgart 1985.
– Karski, Jan, *Story of a Secret State*, The Riverside Press, Cambridge 1944.
– *Keesings Archiv der Gegenwart*, 16th/17th year, Essen 1948.
– Klarsfeld, Beate and Serge, *Le Mémorial de la Déportation des Juifs de France*, Paris 1978.
– Kogon, Eugen, Hermann Langbein and Adalbert Rückerl (ed.), *Nationalsozialistische Massentötungen durch Giftgas*, Fischer Taschenbuch Verlag, Frankfurt 1986.
– Krausnick, Helmut, and Hans-Heinrich Wilhelm, *Die Truppe des Weltanschauungskrieges*, Stuttgart 1981.
– Kulaszka, Barbara, (ed.), *Did Six Million Really Die?*, Samisdat Publishers, Toronto 1992.
– Lambrecht, Wolfgang, "*Zyklon B – eine Ergänzung*", *Vierteljahreshefte für freie Geschichtsforschung*, 1(1) (1997), pp. 2-5.
– Lengyel, Olga, *Five Chimneys*, Chicago/New York 1947.
– Leuchter, Fred A., *An Engineering Report on the Alleged Execution Gas Chambers at Auschwitz, Birkenau and Majdanek, Poland*, Samisdat Publishers, Toronto 1995.
– Marais, Pierre, *Les camions à gaz en question*, Polémiques, Paris 1994.

– Maser, Werner, *Der Wortbruch. Hitler, Stalin und der Zweite Weltkrieg*, Olzog Verlag, Munich 1994.

– Mattogno, Carlo, *Il rapporto Gerstein. Anatomia di un falso*, Sentinella d'Italia, Monfalcone 1985.

   – *La soluzione finale*, Edizioni di Ar, Padua 1991.

   – "*'Schlüsseldokument' – eine alternative Interpretation*", *Vierteljahreshefte für freie Geschichtsforschung*, 4(1) (2000), pp. 51-56

– Müller, Filip, *Eyewitness Auschwitz*, Stein and Day, New York 1979.

   – *Sonderbehandlung*, Steinhausen, Frankfurt 1979.

– Musial, Bogdan, *Konterrevolutionäre Elemente sind zu erschießen*, Propyläen, Berlin 2000.

– Nicosia, Francis, *Hitler und der Zionismus*, Druffel, Leoni 1989.

– Nordling, Carl, "*L'Établissment juif sous la menace et la domination nazies de 1938 à 1945*", *Revue d'Histoire Révisionniste*, no. 2 (1990).

– Nyiszli, Miklos, *Im Jenseits der Menschlichkeit*, Dietz Verlag, Berlin 1992.

– Paul, Allen, *Katyn. The Untold Story of Stalin's Polish Massacre*, Charles Scribner's Sons, New York [2]1991.

– Pawlikowski, Jozef, "*Einige Anmerkungen zu jüdischen Bevölkerungsstatistiken*", *Vierteljahreshefte für freie Geschichtsforschung*, 2(1) (1998), p. 36f.

– Poliakov, Léon, *Harvest of Hate*, Holocaust Library, New York 1979.

– Porter, Carlos W., and Vincent Reynouard, *Menteur à Nuremberg*, ANEC, Paris 1998.

– Post, Walter, *Unternehmen Barbarossa*, Mittler, Hamburg 1995.

– Pressac, Jean-Claude, *Auschwitz. Technique and Operation of the Gas Chambers*, Beate Klarsfeld Foundation, New York 1989.

   – *Les Crématoires d'Auschwitz*, CNRS, Paris 1994.

– Rassinier, Paul, *Le Drame des Juifs européens*, Les Sept Couleurs, Paris 1967, reprinted by La Vieille Taupe, Paris 1984.

   – *Le Mensonge d'Ulysse*, Paris 1950.

– Reder, Rudolf, *Bełżec*, Cracow 1946.

– Reitlinger, Gerald, *The Final Solution. The Attempt to Exterminate the Jews of Europe 1939-1945*, Jason Aronson, Northgate, New Jersey 1987.

– Roques, Henri, *The "Confessions" of Kurt Gerstein*, Institute for Historical Review, Costa Mesa, CA, 1989.

– Rudolf, Germar, *The Rudolf Report*, Theses & Dissertations Press, Capshaw, AL, 2001.

   – and Schröder, Sibylle, "*Partisanenkrieg und Repressaltötungen*", *Vierteljahreshefte für freie Geschichtsforschung*, 3(2) (1999), pp. 145-153.

– Sanning, Walter N., *The Dissolution of the Eastern European Jewry*, Institute for Historical Review, Newport Beach, CA, 1983.

– Schweitzer, Eva, *"Rücksicht auf die Verbündeten. Ein Gespräch mit Raul Hilberg über Norman Finkelsteins Buch 'The Holocaust Industry,'"* Berliner Zeitung, Sept. 4, 2000.

– Seidler, Franz W., *Die Wehrmacht im Partisanenkrieg*, Pour le Mérite, Selent 1998.

– Sereny, Gitta, *Am Abgrund. Eine Gewissensforschung*, Ullstein, Frankfurt 1980.

– Shirer, William L., *Rise and Fall of the Third Reich*, Simon and Schuster, New York, 1960.

– Solschenizyn, Alexander, *Der Archipel Gulag*, Scherz Verlag, Bern 1974.

– Stäglich, Wilhelm, *Auschwitz. A Judge Looks at the Evidence*, 2nd ed., Institute for Historical Review, Costa Mesa, CA, 1990.

– Suhl, Yuri, *Ed essi si ribellarono. Storia della resistenza ebrea contro il nazismo*, Milan 1969.

– Suvorov, Victor, *Icebreaker: Who Started the Second World War?*, Hamish Hamilton, London 1990
  – *Der Tag M*, Klett-Cotta, Stuttgart 1995
  – *Stalins verhinderter Erstschlag*, Pour le Merite, Selente 2000

– Szende, Stefan, *Der letzte Jude aus Polen*, Europa Verlag, Zürich/New York 1945.

– *The Black Book—The Nazi Crime against the Jewish People*, Reprint Nexus Press, New York 1981.

– Topitsch, Ernst, *Stalin's War*, Fourth Estate, London 1987.

– *Trial of Josef Kramer and 44 others (The Belsen Trial)*, William Hodge and Company, London/Edinburgh/Glasgow 1946.

– Robert van Pelt, Deborah Dwork, *Auschwitz: 1270 to the Present*, Yale University Press, New Haven and London 1996.

– Verbeke, Herbert, *Auschwitz: Nackte Fakten*, V.H.O., Berchem 1995.

– Vrba, Rudolf, *I Cannot Forgive*, Bantam, Toronto 1964.

– Walendy, Udo, *"Babi Jar – die Schlucht 'mit 33.711 ermordeten Juden'?"*, in: *Historische Tatsachen* no. 51, Verlag für Volkstum und Zeitgeschichtsforschung, Vlotho 1992.
  – *"Der Fall Treblinka"*, *Historische Tatsachen* no. 44, Verlag für Volkstum und Zeitgeschichtsforschung, Vlotho 1990.

– Wegner, Bernd (ed.), *Zwei Wege nach Moskau*, Piper, Munich 1991.

– Wien, E.R., *Die Shoa von Babi Jar*, Hartung-Gorre, Constance 1991.

– Wiesel, Elie, *Die Nacht zu begraben, Elischa*, Ullstein, Frankfurt 1990.
  – *Night*, Hill and Wang, New York, 1960.

– Wiesenthal, Simon, *Der neue Weg*, Vienna, no. 17/18 and 19/20, 1946.

125

Index of Names

Page numbers in italics indicate occurences in footnotes only.